NEW
DIRECTIONS

SUCCESSFUL STRATEGIES *for* CAREER, *the* WORKPLACE, *and* PERSONAL GROWTH

NEW DIRECTIONS

JAMES G. WARD

GREENLEAF
BOOK GROUP PRESS

Published by Greenleaf Book Group Press
Austin, Texas
www.gbgpress.com

Distributed by Greenleaf Book Group

For ordering information or special discounts for bulk purchases, please contact Greenleaf Book Group at PO Box 91869, Austin, TX 78709, 512.891.6100.

Design and composition by Greenleaf Book Group
Cover design by Greenleaf Book Group

Cataloging-in-Publication data is available.

Print ISBN: 978-1-62634-353-5

eBook ISBN: 978-1-62634-354-2

Part of the Tree Neutral® program, which offsets the number of trees consumed in the production and printing of this book by taking proactive steps, such as planting trees in direct proportion to the number of trees used: www.treeneutral.com

TreeNeutral®

Printed in the United States of America on acid-free paper

16 17 18 19 20 21   10 9 8 7 6 5 4 3 2 1

First Edition

To Carol
Whose love, support, and endurance
helped bring my dream to reality

"The beginning is the most important part of the work."

—Plato, Greek philosopher

Contents

Foreword

Today's global economy requires new skills, talent, and temperament. The rapid pace of change is transforming and redefining job descriptions, career paths, entire industries, and even professions. Against this setting, there are numerous advisors and authors who claim to provide career assistance and counseling. And some of it is quite good.

But I have always found that the most practical professional advice is derived from real-world experience. I call it "situational management." You learn from doing! You create solutions from real problems. And you change tactics from making errors.

Jim Ward's book, *New Directions*, not only provides useful tools for career advice but also views them through a unique lens of experience. I have known and worked with Jim for over twenty years. I have observed him in delicate personal encounters, group confrontations, restructurings, rapid expansion, and a range of other situations. I have a good basis for assessing his talent.

To me this book offers meaningful lessons in *real* world practical answers against a *new* world of challenges in the workplace! It's like listening to a partner! Regardless of your current job prospects and career success, I think you will find Jim's book thought provoking and highly informative.

Bill Thompson
Retired CEO, PIMCO

Why Seek a New Direction?

The only constant in life is change.

—Heraclitus, Greek philosopher

Managing through a long career is hard work. During my thirty-year business career, I have had firsthand experience observing a changing business landscape from the front line. Many of the career myths we have come to believe, such as "The company will always take care of me," no longer apply and are unrealistic. In today's workplace, we must deal with the corporate reality of how a change in management, corporate downsizing, merger, or restructuring can impact us personally. In addition, dealing with a difficult boss can often lead us to seek new employment and/or other career options.

Careers don't just happen. They are planned and adjusted. It's not just the plumbers, bricklayers, and carpenters that need a sound set of tools to optimize their work. Individuals across all walks of life and professions need career tools, which are strategies they can use to make themselves successful.

A new approach and mindset is needed today to survive the ups and downs of a long working career. A profound paradigm shift has occurred in how we define "career" and how we approach the workplace. That is what *New Directions* is all about.

Welcome, and I hope you enjoy my work.

Introduction

The thought behind this book came to me as I was completing almost one year of writing a blog under the title *New Directions* for an online business publication. The blog focused on career and workplace issues, specifically career strategies and mobility, and workplace development and leadership. During the course of the two years I wrote the blog, I received many positive comments from readers, including the following: "Thanks for your marvelous posting!" and "Would you mind if I share your blog with my Twitter group? There are a lot of people [who] would really appreciate your excellent content." Comments like these encouraged me to consider revising those blog posts into a book.

As background, I am a career human resources (HR) executive and professional coach. I've worked in these areas for more than twenty-five years. In that time, I've worked with all levels of employees seeking new directions—from leaders as they dealt with their own career transitions, to midcareer professionals who've been laid off, to young people looking for their very first job after college, and to all sorts of workers in between.

During my own career, I have seen enormous changes in America's business environment from the front line. In the early 1980s, as I started my career, I worked for a global energy services firm as an in-house staff recruiter. We were hiring engineers of all levels across many different engineering disciplines (chemical, petroleum, mechanical, etc.) to gear up for the oil and gas boom that was in its early stages. Suddenly and almost overnight the landscape changed! The oil crisis hit, and we were cutting all those engineers that we had hired with the promise of unlimited opportunity. The oil and gas industry was now in a state of turmoil and was firing significant numbers of staff. There were *no* jobs for these experienced engineers to go to; engineering jobs seemed to evaporate overnight.

Gone were the days when American workers could get a job with one company and work there until they retired. Instead, many of these individuals had to find new careers and transition into entirely new professional endeavors. Difficult as it was dealing with this tragedy and sorrow, it was a tremendous opportunity for me to gain insight and experience into coaching these individuals, particularly by helping them explore alternative ways to find employment.

I again experienced this same situation during the financial crisis of 2007–2008, when the world experienced the worst financial crisis since the Great Depression. Investors and policy makers throughout the world confronted the painful economic consequences arising from the meltdown in the US mortgage market. In a short period of time, the world was on the brink of financial collapse. Wealth was destroyed around the globe, organizations began to draw down on their lines of credit, and consumer confidence was decimated. Suddenly, the major banks (Lehman Brothers, Bear Sterns, Countrywide Financial, etc.) were bankrupt. The federal government had to step in and rescue many of these failing banks.

Financial services professionals were out of work en masse. Unemployment climbed to over ten percent. However, the unemployment rate was significantly higher for the chronically unemployed—those who'd already quit looking for work. During this period of time, I was the global head of human resources for Pacific Investment Management Company (PIMCO), an investment management firm specializing in fixed-income asset management. Ironically, our business was growing then, as many of the large pension plans were moving assets to the safety of fixed-income investments from equities. We continued to hire during this time. The massive layoffs going on in the financial services sector meant we were bombarded with resumes from professionals looking for work. Thousands upon thousands of financial services professionals were struggling to find work. We advertised for a vice president/senior credit analyst and received more than *seven hundred* resumes, all from qualified applicants. Many of these individuals would not work again in their chosen field. I found myself in the role of coach, mentor, and advisor to many individuals looking to transition.

These days, because of the changes in the business landscape, it's critical that workers be willing and able to transition into new jobs—sometimes into new careers. The pages in this book will help everyone from the first-time employee, to the midcareer shifter, to the peak earner who wants an even harder challenge.

We spend half our lives working. We deserve to spend that time in work we enjoy—work that draws on our strengths and interests.

I hope you enjoy my thoughts and insights. As you polish your resume and perfect your online job-search profile, remember this, above all else:

In work, we have the possibility of discovering ourselves.

—Anonymous

Careers in Today's World

You've got to be careful if you don't know where you're going, because you might not get there.

—Yogi Berra, baseball legend

What Is a Career?

It doesn't happen all at once [that] you become.
It takes a long time.

—Margery Williams, *The Velveteen Rabbit*

Douglas Hall, in his book *Careers in Organizations*, defined a career as a "lifelong sequence of role-related experiences."[1] A traditional view of "career" is paternal, providing stability and direction. Prior to the Second World War, and shortly thereafter, workers' careers were simpler to manage because control was in the hands of the employer. There was generally one employer and one career field across a person's life span. Hard work paid off through retirement.

Today, we know that the new realities of managing our careers are more complicated. Often we see individuals having multiple careers in their lifetime, which can span different fields of endeavor altogether. This process can be carefully planned or simply managed haphazardly. Regardless of the individual circumstances, this process can lead to personal fulfillment or be totally frustrating. The cyclical nature of the global economy requires us to think about work and career differently. Since the 1970s, managing a career has become much more complex and difficult, due in part to globalization, rapid changes in technology, and economic turbulence.

The rise in alternative work arrangements has become part of the current employment landscape.

As a result of all this change, we have experienced the death of the psychological contract between employer and employee. The concept of "lifetime employment" is essentially dead. Employees now work for and with multiple employers over their working careers.

Donald Super was an early pioneer in the field of career development and one of the first thought leaders to do serious research on the subject. In one of his many research articles, "Career Development Theory," he outlined his career model, which was based on the belief that a person's self-concept changes over time and develops as a result of that person's lifelong experiences. Super's theory of career development identified five stages—growth stage, exploration stage, establishment stage, maintenance stage, and decline stage—that individuals go through; and as we mature, our vocational maturity increases with age. Careers could be conceptualized in stages:

- **Growth stage** (birth to age 14): Developing self-concept, attitudes, and understanding of work. Parental influence is important.

- **Exploration stage** (ages 15–24): Exploration of interests and career possibilities through education and hobbies.

- **Establishment stage** (ages 25–44): Acquisition of skills, experience, and expertise becoming established in a given field.

- **Maintenance stage** (ages 45–64): Maintaining job security and continuously making adjustments to improve position. Career advancement strategies.

- **Decline stage** (ages 65+): Decreased output, preparing for retirement. Disengagement from the workforce.[2]

In addition, we know that in our thirties and forties unique changes can take place in our lives—for example, the way our personal lives become more important. Starting a family can have an effect on this change in focus. All of this can lead to a new and different view of career. At some point, workers reach plateaus; when this happens, climbing the hierarchy of the corporate ladder may no longer be the goal. Today we are seeing a profound paradigm shift in how we view our relationship to work. Members of the millennial generation—those born in the 1980s and 1990s—want a better work-life balance, and often prefer to be self-employed to allow greater flexibility. Simply put, this generation is no longer putting the company before all else in life.

What has replaced the organizational men and women of yesteryear? The self-managed career has; these days you are in charge of and control your career direction.

The Self-Managed Career

Choose your career not on the basis
of what you know, but who you are.
—Anonymous

The self-managed career has replaced the traditional view of work; individuals now have greater control over their own destiny. To a certain degree, employees now regard themselves as free agents. Douglas Hall has written extensively on the new career contract, beginning with his 1976 book *Careers in Organizations*. He further developed his theory in his research paper "The Protean Career: A Quarter-Century Journey." Hall coined the concept of the "protean" career, named for the Greek god Proteus, who was able to fluidly transform his shape to avoid revealing what he knew and who he was. The protean career is one "in which the person, not the organization, is in charge."[3] This new concept of personal career management means the worker is continuously learning, remains open to new possibilities, and has the potential for multiple careers and occupations over a lifetime.

Today's workers are in charge of themselves. The emotional gains resulting from the new definition of career are greater self-reliance, a feeling of empowerment, and an enhanced sense of self-worth. Individuals accepting the new self-managed career definition typically seek jobs that suit their core values and passions and that offer greater personal flexibility and work-life balance.

What does all of this mean in terms of the right career strategy? Does it mean you are to be self-serving, blindly and opportunistically moving from one employer to another? No, what I am saying is to be mindful and prepared. Organizational loyalty is important. However, don't put one hundred percent of your faith in the organization to take care of you. Take control of your career! Adhere to the self-managed career definition. The profound changes in the business climate over the past twenty-five years require us to think differently about ourselves, our careers, and how to navigate organizational ambiguity. A recent Gallup research report showed that seventy percent of US workers were not engaged at work (i.e., not happy or satisfied with their employer or career choice).[4] This is a staggering statistic. All the more reason to adopt a new way of thinking about your career. It's more important to be engaged and satisfied with your work than to spend thirty years in a job you hate or a career you are unhappy with.

Career Choices

We can change our lives.
We can do, have, and be exactly what we wish.

—**Anthony Robbins,** American motivational speaker and author

Career choices are easy, right? Not so fast! Choosing which job to take is easy compared to choosing a career. It's the age-old chicken-or-the-egg dilemma—which comes first, the job or the career? For example, you can't have a career without having a job, and there's no job worth having that isn't part of a career. Many of us would see a job flipping burgers at the local fast-food restaurant as not worth having, unless you had a clear path to becoming a store manager or multi-unit manager.

We may tend to think of our career choice as a lifelong commitment, but the reality is that in today's world we often have a series of mini-careers over our lifetimes. This realization might put less pressure on individuals as they think about what "to do for a living," but some pressure still exists. Although you may have studied to be an accountant, engineer, teacher, and so on, you may find you need to take a new direction. Career uncertainty is a common occurrence. It was not that long ago that once you chose your field of study, you were on a direct path to a lifelong profession. High school and college students today are faced with this important decision of what to do for a career, vocation, or trade. Hopefully today's college placement offices offer more support and realistic direction than they did when I graduated. For years the Department of Labor published its annual *Dictionary of Occupation Titles*, which highlighted thousands of available occupations. I remember the placement office giving me this book to review during my college days. That was the extent of their advice! This publication has now been replaced with the Occupational Information Network database (https://www.onetonline.org/). Individuals today have unlimited online resources to help bring clarity to the topic of career choice and options. In addition, today there are a number of good psychometric tools available to use to guide individuals as to their interest, occupational skills, and career orientation. Recent news articles tell us there is a renewed interest in and premium placed on technical skills, and vocations requiring skills training are on the rise. In many cases, students are staying off the path to college and opting instead to gain vocational training.

Following your passion and interest, in my view, is the most important aspect of career choice. It doesn't matter what you choose as a career—doctor, lawyer, nurse, plumber, welder, teacher, or farmer. The important thing to know is we do have choices! Remember the adage "Do what you love, and you will never work a day in your life." This should be your goal as you ponder your career choices.

PASSION AT ITS CORE: NOAH

A long-term friend of mine recently confided in me that he was concerned about his son's overall direction in life. His son, Noah, had studied music in college and was not able to make a career in the music industry. His father was anxious because he felt Noah was on a dead-end path. Noah had held a series of low-end restaurant positions and was in his early thirties. My friend wanted me to meet with Noah, which I was happy to do. During several meetings, I listened and probed as to Noah's goals and ideas about what he wanted to do with his work and career. I found Noah to be a person with passion, drive, and obvious talent.

Although Noah's career trajectory was not obvious to his father, Noah did have a plan. His seemingly low-end restaurant positions provided him with insight into the restaurant business and contacts he would later need to achieve his goals. He told me that he had been studying to become a master sommelier, because there are multiple phases to this process and it can take years to achieve. One must pass each stage and exam before progressing to the next level. Noah was very realistic about the study of wine and what it would ultimately lead to in terms of career choice. He was also realistic about the types of career options, particularly the nontraditional hours often associated with this line of work. Noah was not the typical nine to five–type guy.

After completing his final sommelier exam, some eight months later, Noah was able to secure a position with an exclusive private country club as the head sommelier. The position paid well and offered good benefits. While this career choice may not fit the "traditional view," it was what Noah wanted for himself. He was successful at turning his passion into reality. His father was relieved that his son was now on a career path.

Career Planning

A winner has a healthy appreciation of his abilities
and a keen awareness of his limitations.

—**Sydney J. Harris,** noted American journalist and author

Career planning is a tricky business. While absolutely necessary to having a successful and long-term career, the planning phase must be approached with eyes wide open. Most importantly, career planning should be done in concert with setting short- and long-term objectives. Often this planning takes place over a significant period of time. And occasionally, careers just happen; and as a result of a series of haphazard events, we find ourselves doing what we are doing.

From the time we plan for college until the day we plan for retirement (or re-direction, as I like to refer to it), career planning is part of our everyday lives. In thinking about career planning, there are five essential components to approaching the subject in the right way:

- First, whatever your chosen endeavor, **commitment is paramount**; you will never be successful at anything unless you are committed.

- Second, **know your strengths and weaknesses**. Without a realistic picture of your skills, strengths, and capabilities, you will fail.

- Third, **the willingness to take risks is important**. In my coaching practice, I always encourage individuals to take a few calculated career risks. It's all about getting out of your comfort zone.

- Fourth, **flexibility is important to maintaining perspective**. The ability to flex to a specific situation, organization, and/or role is important.

- Last, the key to any form of career planning is to **always have a backup plan**. Prepare for the unexpected. When things don't work out as you planned or hoped, have a "plan B" in place and ready to go. The important thing is not to get caught flat-footed and without an exit strategy.

FINDING THE INTERSECTION
OF MULTIPLE INTERESTS: STEPHANIE

Stephanie, a recent college graduate, graduated at the top of her class in premed. She had taken the entrance exam to get into medical school, and scored in the top ten percent. Stephanie was in the process of applying to medical schools when she decided she did not want to go into medicine! She never got those applications off. Stephanie loved medicine, but she did not have the stomach for years of educational debt. Moreover, Stephanie passionately wanted to be a surgeon, but a recent serious hand injury would prevent that. She needed to adjust her plans. Many of today's college graduates have a similar story. Their career plans change after graduation.

Stephanie had worked in many different restaurants during college and worked weekends as a bartender. So she decided to become a full-time bartender and did that for the next three years, while trying to figure out which direction to take.

During this time she started taking business classes and eventually enrolled in an executive MBA program at a top-tier school. Stephanie's focus in business school was to bridge her interest in business with her interest in medicine. She wanted to figure out where those two fields intersected.

I was referred to Stephanie by a mutual friend and had several coaching sessions with her. After some psychometric testing, I discovered that one of her strengths was her outgoing personality. Stephanie was engaging and assertive, someone who had no fear of failure and displayed tremendous resiliency. After she graduated from business school, Stephanie began to explore medical sales. She interviewed with several organizations and found it to be extremely competitive, which did not dissuade her at all. The more research she did, the more she thought medical sales was the right career path to pursue. After months of an aggressive job search, Stephanie was offered a position in medical sales with a Fortune 500 medical device manufacturer. This organization manufactured medical devices for orthopedic surgeons, which allowed Stephanie to put her knowledge of medicine to practical use. In her role, she sold directly to doctors and was required to observe actual surgeries to advise the surgeon on the proper methods to insert these medical devices. Stephanie found a way to intersect both of her interests—business and medicine—while also putting to use her sales-oriented personality.

Contents of Your "New Directions" Toolbox

When we are no longer able to change a situation,
we are challenged to change ourselves.

—**Viktor E. Frankl,** author of *Man's Search for Meaning*

Recently, I found myself rereading Marshall Goldsmith's wonderful book *What Got You Here Won't Get You There.* I use this book a great deal in my coaching practice. When I think about goals, I think of the interesting challenge Goldsmith poses at the end of his book. He asks readers to imagine they are ninety-five years of age and on their deathbed. Before taking their last breath, they have the ability to reach back in time and speak to their younger selves. Think about this now: Having the benefit of time and experience, what advice would you give yourself about being a better professional and a better person? In essence, what have you learned in those ninety-five years with regard to professional and personal experiences? I frequently ask my clients this question, and they struggle to find an answer. Interestingly, I recently asked my very healthy, not-near-his-deathbed ninety-two-year-old father-in-law this very question. He responded that he wished he had been a better communicator. The rest, in theory, is easy. Act on the basis of the advice you would give to your younger self. Simple, right?

This is a great exercise to go through as we plan for New Directions in our career. Following the economic turbulence of 2007–2008, we are seeing an improving economy, which brings hope to us all. It opens up new possibilities. It's time to find your passion and do it. If you are unhappy with your current job/career/boss, then make a detailed plan to change it. What career and personal goals have you set for yourself? Planning for change takes time; it does not just happen.

Envision a plan for yourself, set a course of action, and stay on track. Expect bumps in the road. Our career often does not progress through a straight, linear path. If we expect potential obstacles in the process, then we are better able to navigate them. As you think about your "New Directions" toolbox, it's helpful to put things into a career timeline. As we learned from Donald Super's career stages, during each phase of our career, our priorities change and are fundamentally different. Early in your career, continuing education and new skills development are critical. Later in life, as you enter the "maintenance stage," these goals might be less of a focus, and the priorities may be career advancement, improving your financial position, and long-term wealth accumulation.

Finally, as you process through the various stages of life and career, don't forget to take time for yourself. Whatever your hobby, take it to the next level. If you are a runner, then run that 5K/10K, or perhaps a marathon. Annually set one personal goal and go for it. It will empower you.

Like the Army: Be, Know, Do

Know thyself.

—Ancient Greek aphorism

Socrates, along with many of his contemporaries, was famous for arguing that one must know "thyself" to be wise. He was really on to something here! He also said, "An unexamined life is not worth living." This concept has important implications for us as we think about developing an effective job-search strategy. You, and you alone, are responsible for guiding your career, its direction, and its progress. This principle underlies the basis of our new understanding of career.

Frances Hesselbein and General Eric K. Shinseki collaboratively adapted *Be, Know, Do: Leadership the Army Way*, and in the introduction to their book, they state, "Field Manual 22–100, *Army Leadership*, has three words on its cover: 'Be, Know, Do.' The US Army has long employed the motto 'Be, Know, Do' in their leadership-training model."[5] This time-honored principle forms the backbone of the army's training philosophy to develop leaders of character, passion, and competence. What does it mean to be, know, and do? To *be* denotes understanding of your self, character, and values; to *know* is to discern your strengths, weaknesses, and skills. To *do* is to take action. These three words and the demands they evoke are relevant to any individual preparing to plan and execute a job search or career change.

In terms of leadership development, the US military wrote the book. Dating back to the early 1950s, many organizations adapted and modeled their leadership training after the military—General Electric being one of the first. My three-phased career-launch strategy is modeled after the Be, Know, Do military formula. How does this motto correlate to an effective career strategy? Where is the intersection? In my mind, this simple army philosophy best describes the kind of rigor, patience, and stick-to-itiveness needed to approach and execute a career-launch strategy and plan. Persistence, courage, and mental toughness go hand in hand with the planning and execution required. Without these attributes, prepare to fail.

Career Launch—Phase 1: Be

Be yourself; everyone else is already taken.

—**Oscar Wilde,** Irish playwright, novelist, and poet

Phase 1 of my career-launch strategy begins with knowing who you are—your strengths, weaknesses, skills, and abilities. How does this work? First, begin by doing an inventory of your work experiences to date. List your significant achievements. Make an inventory of those specific accomplishments for each job you have had. Throughout this process of self-inventory, identify your strengths and weaknesses. Strengths are something at which you excel. The achievements you list should include one or more of your strengths. For example, the ability to troubleshoot and solve problems quickly should be considered a strength. A weakness is a development area, and we all have them. For example, wanting to make better presentations is an improvement you can work on. We should have a plan in place to improve on our weaknesses.

This self-assessment will lead to a better understanding of who you are, but more importantly, it will lead to a better understanding of what you want from your next position. This preparation phase cannot be underestimated. Devote time to this phase. In the end, it will pay off. It works regardless of whether you are a recent college graduate, senior manager, or midcareer professional in transition. Mastering this phase will also help you as you start interviewing and selling yourself to potential employers. It may seem tedious and boring at first, but believe me, based on my personal experience, individuals who truly know who they are come across with much more self-confidence.

According to Richard Bolles, author of *What Color Is Your Parachute?*, individuals "who fail to find their dream job fail not because they lack information about the job market, but because they lack information about themselves."[6]

Career Launch—Phase 2: Know

If you want to be happy, put your effort into
controlling the sail, not the wind.

—Anonymous

Taking control of the "sail" is taking control of your job search and career change. Now that you have mastered the art of self-discovery as outlined in phase 1, it's time to move on to the "know" phase of my career-launch model. What does it mean to know? This phase is all about educating yourself and knowing your market and industry focus, specifically what organizations you want to target. It's the **preparation**, **research**, and **planning** phase. Doing the research to gather all the relevant information is key to your success. So, how do you get started?

First, make a list of all the organizations you are interested in, including a list of organizations across many different industry sectors. This list should be extensive. The old sales philosophy of knowing the product before attempting to sell it also applies to your job search. In order to distinguish between job leads that are useful and leads that are not, you must know the market, industry, and sector you want to target.

The next step is to identify primary contacts you may have within these organizations, or secondary contacts you may have that know individuals within your list of organizations. It's all about networking! As a social networking tool, LinkedIn is invaluable here. The more contacts you make, the better. These contacts are a tremendous source of information. This "contact network" is your real pipeline to success.

This process is all about developing your marketing campaign and strategy. It includes not only market identification but also methods of approach, or "how to" strategies, such as upgrading your resume to fit specific career options and situations, interview preparation, and, finally, salary negotiation, or "closing."

Phase 2 is comprehensive and time intensive.

Let's face it—research is research and can be monotonous. Phase 2 requires patience and determination. Don't underestimate the commitment required for success.

Career Launch—Phase 3: Do

If you have always done it that way, it is probably wrong.

—**Charles Kettering,** American inventor

When I think about launching an effective job search or career change, this quote resonates with me. The old adage "If it ain't broke, don't fix it" is outdated in today's highly competitive world and will leave you "in the dust," as described in the book *If It Ain't Broke . . . Break It!* by Robert Kriegel and Louis Patler. Passion, creativity, and imagination are critical to the job search, which leads to phase 3 of my career-launch strategy. To "do" is to execute.

Taking everything you did in phase 1 and phase 2 and putting it all into action is the bottom line for phase 3. It's the *do*, the action strategy, which internalizes all the work on self from phase 1 and implements the action strategies from the research conducted during phase 2. The most important aspect of this final phase is to effectively use the concepts you developed from your earlier work.

At this point you should have created your own unique "brand" of who you are, and it's time to sell yourself. Beginning to make calls to introduce yourself in the right way is critical to using your contacts effectively. Often you will have less than sixty seconds to get your message across to create a memorable introduction. Practice this with someone; role-play it. It's important.

The next thing to understand is how to develop and maximize the "informational interview" to gain important intelligence and make valuable connections. What is the informational interview? Reaching out to contacts to seek their valuable insight and professional advice. This is a key component to developing your own professional brand and communicating with the business community about your goals and objectives. Used effectively, these types of informational interviews will lead to positive referrals and, most importantly, allow you to communicate with many different people on a professional level, thus heightening your chances for success.

At this juncture, you have put it all together—career-launch phases 1, 2, and 3.

Who's Seeking Work?

Great things are not done by impulse, but by a series of small things together. And great things are not accidental, but must certainly be willed.

—Vincent van Gogh, Dutch impressionist painter

Who Needs a New Direction?

In the middle of difficulty lies opportunity.

—**John Wheeler,** discussing Albert Einstein's work

The simple answer—we all do! As we enter the workforce and progress through our careers, strategies and plans need to change. Experience, tenure, and acquired skills all play significant roles in determining and shaping our career direction.

I look at career planning as a "spectrum" exercise; where you are on that spectrum determines how you plan. Are you just beginning your career? Are you a midcareer professional thinking about a job change? New graduates face challenges specific to their age and education, and uncertainty about their interests and opportunities. Our perspectives and priorities change as we mature from entry level to midcareer to retirement—and so do the tools we need in our career toolbox. A career plan that worked for a newly minted college graduate is not the right one for someone with ten years' experience.

In fact, career plans that worked for most job seekers ten years ago have also changed; old rules regarding career planning no longer apply in today's employment market. Just as life is a journey, so too is a career. We are all on a journey, even individuals who are completely happy with their jobs, employers, and places in life— theirs is a journey of self-discovery and improvement. Learning new skills and keeping up to date with developments in your field of endeavor are part of that journey.

How many of us would choose to go to a physician who hasn't cracked open a medical textbook since medical school, attended a medical conference, or researched the latest report on multiple drug interactions? No one! We all should be working at developing ourselves, to be better at what we do, regardless of whether we are actively seeking new work or simply exploring new directions in our lives.

My message is this: **Expand your career by expanding your knowledge base, skills, and expertise.** If you follow this advice, you'll be on a course of continuous self-improvement. You'll enjoy your life's journey even more. Why is that? For one, as we learn new skills and develop our capabilities, our opportunities will expand significantly, which will lead to personal fulfillment.

Today, we are seeing a changing and expanding definition of "career." Holding multiple part-time jobs is more common; in fact, it may be the norm in the future. Perhaps you're a spin class instructor and also a personal trainer. It does not matter what you choose to do; the spectrum exercise is an excellent way to look at your current situation and plan for the future. If you choose to have multiple part-time positions, be strategic about them and choose ones with a clear career trajectory in mind. As you grow, mature, and develop from a work and career perspective, where do you want to be in five years, ten years, and beyond? Where are you on your career "spectrum"?

Our Journey on the Career Spectrum

A journey of a thousand miles begins with a single step.

—Lao-Tzu, *Tao Te Ching*

There are many career stages we go through as we progress through life. In thinking about those stages, and to simplify them, I have broken the list into four primary groups:

- **First job**
  - Just out of college or high school
  - Looking for part-time work while a student
  - Looking for summer internships during college

- **Early career:** Ages—twenties to thirties
  - Finishing grad school
  - Looking for radical shift between industries
  - Seeking change within same industry or company

- **Midcareer:** Ages—thirties to forties
  - Stepping out of established career, ready to try something new
  - Needing to leave unpleasant/impossible work environment
  - Quitting your boss, not the company
  - Bad fit with new management
  - Seeking to re-enter the workforce after parenting or caregiving
  - Leveraging your earning potential

- **Late career:** Ages—fifties to seventies

- Launching businesses. Exploring something entrepreneurial
- Consulting
- Ratcheting down to part-time employment
- Terminated and devastated

Career Stagnation

It is good to have an end to journey toward;
but it is the journey that matters, in the end.
—**Ursula K. Le Guin,** *The Left Hand of Darkness*

Have you ever felt like you were in a career rut? You just didn't like your job or your boss, or you felt little satisfaction in what you were doing? You're not alone! Perhaps you are suffering from career stagnation. The good news is we have all been there at one point in our careers. If you are unhappy with your current job, chosen profession, or career choice, perhaps it's time to plan a change. The right change may involve a minor tweak here or there, or it may encompass a complete overhaul. Regardless, if you are feeling "the blahs," start by taking a complete inventory of what's going on.

Conducting a thorough self-audit or self-evaluation is the right place to begin. Try to pinpoint the problem or issue. What is the source of your frustration? Feeling underappreciated, underpaid, or underutilized within your organization can lead to career stagnation. Perhaps part of the solution may be as simple as changing your routine. How do you organize your day or spend your time at work? Look for ways to change things up. Simple adjustments can go a long way in improving your situation.

However, if your career stagnation is the result of a much bigger issue, take the time to think about the correct course of action. Changing jobs, changing career direction, or moving to a new city to start over can all be rewarding life events; but they should not be taken lightly. These types of transitions take planning and careful thought. They require that you have a vision, take time to plan, and work out a strategy. You may want to speak with a mentor, coach, or professional confidant you trust and respect. Getting advice and guidance from others can help you feel not only more prepared but also less alone.

Day-to-day frustrations do happen, so I find it's helpful if you remember to laugh a little. The rut is not as bad with a sense of humor.

MIDCAREER JOB SHIFT: ANN

Ann was a successful financial services investment professional with an undergraduate degree from UCLA and an MBA from NYU. She started her career in equity trading and spent a number of years in equity research, eventually moving into money management as a portfolio manager, where she managed a multimillion-dollar equity portfolio for a large hedge fund. The problem: She hated her job and the stress that comes with managing other people's money. The part of her job that was most troubling was using leverage to make large bets, both short and long positions, on stock movements. She lost a great deal of sleep over this. It was just not in her DNA.

Ann had long been interested in the financial aspects of running a business. She was very interested in pursuing the role of CFO for a midsized organization. As I worked with Ann, we tried to identify aspects of her background that could be translated to the skills a CFO needs. First, her undergraduate degree was in accounting. She had also assumed a significant role as a volunteer with a large national nonprofit organization. I suggested she seek the treasurer role for this organization to get some actual experience in managing profit-and-loss statements and balance sheets for this nonprofit. She was able to make that happen, which gave her the solid, practical experience she needed.

The next phase of her transition involved targeting the right industry sector that played to her knowledge of financial services. After breaking this down to industry verticals and specific organizations, she homed in on midsized private equity organizations and large family offices with significant investment platforms, both of which played to her industry background and knowledge.

These steps worked. Today Ann is the CFO of a large multifamily office. She no longer has sleepless nights; she is in a role she enjoys and for which she has a passion.

Transitions: Letting Go and Moving On

Before you can begin something new,
you have to end what used to be.

—**William Bridges,** change management authority
and author of *Managing Transitions*

Professionals from all walks of life can find themselves in a position of career transition. Have you ever been downsized, or rightsized, or been terminated as a result of a political triangle gone bad? Those of you who've experienced this will never forget that sickening feeling in the pit of your stomach when you are called to the HR office and told you no longer have a job!

Individuals experiencing this need for a "new direction" in life are often at a loss as to how to begin. As a starting point, anyone in this situation must psychologically let go of the past in order to move forward. More than anything, transitions are internal. Losing your job as a result of a corporate restructuring or being let go due to conflicts with your boss are not situations to be embarrassed or humiliated about. It happens! Transitions begin by first letting go; the next step is taking action and moving forward.

For many reasons, this process is not an easy one. Unfortunately, we often become content in situations in which we find ourselves, even if we are unhappy. Today, because of the past economic turmoil and job loss, individuals are financially and emotionally so invested with their employer that any disruption, or even the possibility of change, threatens their sense of safety. In reality, change is often just the thing we need to get us going. What I've seen in my experience as a career coach is that individuals going through transitions almost always end up in better places than they were before. However, from an emotional and psychological perspective, understanding this can take some time.

Transitions allow us to step back, take inventory, and begin again. A linear path no longer identifies careers. There will be bumps in the road. Understanding how to deal with these bumps, start over, and, ultimately, recycle yourself is important. Pamela McLean and Frederic Hudson, in their book *LifeLaunch*, introduce the concept of "the endless change rule." Changes in life and in your career are inevitable. They're also ongoing and endless. Managing this uncertainty forms part of our ability to learn, grow, and change. Most importantly, you need to take an honest inventory of what you did that may have contributed to this sudden change.

We live in a world of uncertainty. Career management is more complicated than it once was. It puts a great deal of responsibility on us as individuals—as free agents, so to speak—to plan, manage, and redirect. Change happens: the new boss, the new project team, the layoff, the new job, and the like. In dealing with transitions, we first need to let go so we can take the appropriate action.

What actions will you take today as you begin your journey through transition? First, take a few steps back and use the time to reflect on *who* you are and *what* you want to do—like the army's "be and know" from section 1. In my current coaching practice and prior corporate career as an HR executive, I've dealt with many different types of professionals going through some kind of transition. My approach in addressing these situations always begins with self-assessment and a look inward. What do you want to do? How do you currently use the skills and talents you already have? How can you transfer these skills and talents to something else you would like and want to do?

Unconscious assumptions often get in the way of our ability to change. Most of us need to be open to taking some career risks by pursuing what we have a passion for and enjoy. Transitions occur throughout our lifetime—some will be relatively minor, while others will be major life changers. Experts tell us that dealing with the loss of a job can be as distressing as dealing with a sudden death or divorce. Regardless, in any transition, self-awareness, self-assessment, and introspection are important.

As you deal with these events, it's important to embrace the insights you've gained from this self-assessment phase. There are no shortcuts to success; desire, motivation, and the will to think differently will create a successful and winning formula. In the end, as you successfully master these different transitions, you will gain confidence, autonomy, and a newfound tolerance for ambiguity.

There is an old saying, "If you don't like the picture, change the frame." This simple phrase is important to embrace as you begin your journey.

Is it time to change the frame?

THE BOOMERANG TRANSITION: DON

Don is a running friend of mine. We often train together for different events. Over the years, he has confided in me about his career struggles. Don has been in sales his entire career, selling outdoor/lifestyle sports equipment, footwear, and apparel. For seventeen years he had been vice president of sales and marketing for a large brand-name manufacturer. He had grown tired of corporate politics and the cyclical nature of the business. One day, he told me he was exploring other opportunities because he was in a career rut. A friend of his was starting a business as a sink manufacturer and needed a partner with sales and marketing expertise. This entrepreneurial opportunity was a complete startup and had significant risks. While they had a manufacturing facility established in China, they were starting fresh, right out of the gate in creating a distribution network for the product in the United States.

They had investors already backing the business, but Don knew his initial compensation would be significantly lower than what he had been making in his corporate position. He was given an ownership stake in the business. So, Don accepted the position. Don spent two years trying to build this business and make it work. At the end of the two years, they were beginning to see results and were slowly moving into becoming profitable.

However, Don was not happy. He found it exceedingly difficult to establish himself in a completely new market and product line, as well as to be in competition with the major sink manufacturers. He was a small fish in a very big pond.

As an active outdoor person who enjoyed running and cycling, he missed the joy he previously had selling in the outdoor active lifestyle market. He made the difficult decision to go back to what he knew and enjoyed. The one thing Don discovered in his brief transition to business owner was that he enjoyed the entrepreneurial aspects of running his own business. He decided to start his own company, operating as an independent representative for several outdoor apparel and sporting goods equipment manufacturers. He ended up with six different product lines to wholesale throughout the western region of the United States.

Don's boomerang transition brought him back to where he started, but on his own terms, sans the corporate politics.

Those Who Have Been Terminated

You're going to like the way you look. I guarantee it.

—**George Zimmer,** American entrepreneur

After forty years at the Men's Wearhouse, George Zimmer was fired. Just like that! Gone! As the face of this organization, and after countless television commercials, he was outright fired. How does this happen, you ask? After his termination, Zimmer spoke about how traumatized he felt. He was quoted as saying, "When I was terminated, I got no severance. They even took my phone and cut off my insurance."[1] Harsh, I'd say.

Even wealthy founders lose their jobs. Go figure. In thinking about this situation, I'm reminded that there is no job security any longer. In reality, we all work for ourselves, free agents to work where we want. This is the new career reality. Career stability has been redefined; the self-managed career has replaced the traditional view. My father-in-law lived a comfortable corporate life, thirty-five years as a geologist at Exxon, joining right out of graduate school. That just does not happen anymore—or happens seldom, anyway. The profound changes in the business climate over the past thirty years require us to think differently about career and how to manage that career.

Is your career on track? Is it time to redirect into something new and different? Taking a career inventory can be insightful, but also smart. It can help you focus on areas of strength or weakness and be a starting point if and when you are hit with an out-of-the-blue event like Zimmer's termination. Make a list of positives and negatives about where you are in your career. It may provide the lift you need to make changes for the better.

WHEN BEING LAID OFF
LEADS TO A NEW DIRECTION: NEIL

During the 1980s economic downturn, oil and energy service organizations were laying off professional engineers (of all specialties) en masse. Mechanical, chemical, and petroleum engineers found themselves out of work and with few options because every company was cutting staff. Those who were the poorest performers were laid off first. Ironically, they occasionally fared better than those who were laid off later, because they ended up getting offers before hiring came to a screeching halt. As more and more layoffs occurred, there were fewer and fewer jobs for these professionals.

During this time, I worked in HR at a very large energy services organization and was tasked with the responsibility of executing the massive layoffs. Just a few short years earlier, we had been recruiting large numbers, and now we were laying off the people we had wooed. This was not an easy role.

I recall one individual who was let go; let's call him Neil. He was a senior project manager and was in charge of a large group of chemical engineers responsible for the design of a multimillion-dollar oil refinery project. The project was shelved, and the entire staff on this project, including Neil, was laid off.

I spent a great deal of time with Neil helping him think through different avenues he could take to find employment to support his family. Well educated with both a bachelor's and master's degree in chemical engineering, he was certain he could find employment with another firm in his chosen profession. He was also willing to relocate, which he believed would expand his universe of opportunities. But after a year of looking, Neil was having very little success at even getting interviews. The global recession had hit hard, and unemployment was in the double digits. Neil was like so many others in the oil industry; he simply could not find a job.

I developed a friendship with Neil. We ended up socializing with our families on many occasions. During dinner at his house one night, I asked Neil whether he'd ever considered exploring work that was more entrepreneurial, like owning a business. As we discussed this further, he told me he sold encyclopedias during graduate school and always enjoyed sales. Neil was outgoing and engaging. He loved to talk, and he never met someone with whom he couldn't find common ground to engage in conversation.

At this point, Neil had a willingness to take a calculated risk—as the old adage goes, "Nothing ventured, nothing gained." He had been given a generous severance package when he was laid off and still had enough of a nest egg that he was willing to consider investing in a franchise opportunity. Neil was an experienced project team leader. I was confident in his ability as an effective strategist who was assertive and had the ability to motivate others, provide direction, and achieve goals—all-important qualities for a successful entrepreneur. He began by developing a step-by-step, systematic plan to reach his goals. As simple as this may sound, Neil did explore this further and ended up becoming an independent agent for a large insurance organization. He ultimately had a very successful career as an insurance sales executive. Over time, Neil opened multiple offices in several cities.

It can take time to reinvent yourself. However, it is possible, and it happens more frequently than you might imagine. Sometimes it takes a traumatic event like the loss of a job for us to see our full potential. Neil's is a case in point: Change can end up being a positive event in your life.

WHEN LOSING ONE JOB RESULTS IN GAINING TWO: STEVE

Steve, a coaching client of mine, was a very successful financial services executive working for a large multibillion-dollar investment bank. Steve was in his early forties and went to work for this organization right after graduating from business school. In addition to his MBA, Steve was an accomplished macroeconomist. During his tenure with this organization, he held numerous positions in sales, trading, and investment banking. He even took an international posting to Hong Kong, where he managed the investment banking team in Asia. When the financial crisis hit in 2007–2008, Steve was en route back to the United States to the home office, because his five-year assignment was up. Soon Steve transitioned into a new role within the organization, but he felt his skills were underutilized. He was also caught up in a political squeeze with his new boss, and when the organization began to cut staff as a result of the financial crisis, Steve was selected for layoff; this, to say the least, devastated him! He found himself at a complete loss as to what to do next.

Steve had always been a top-tier performer. This was at the height of the financial crisis, and similar positions were difficult to find, even with his credentials and background. Moreover, this negative experience caused him to completely change his mind about working for another financial services organization. The trauma of losing his job after almost twenty years at this organization was an emotional pivot-point for Steve.

Steve had always maintained a relationship with the business school he graduated from. He was still making appearances as a guest lecturer there, and sat on the school's investment committee. As I worked with Steve during this transition, it became clear to me that his next career move should involve teaching.

Steve eventually concluded that teaching was the right option for him to pursue. He enjoyed the role of teacher and felt energized when working with students who were interested in financial services as a career. Steve had a great deal to offer. The remaining hurdles were logistical and financial. He was offered an opportunity at the business school he graduated from, but it required him to relocate. Moreover, compensation was an issue. Professors are not paid what corporate executives are paid, particularly financial services executives. His solution? He decided to relocate, and accepted the teaching position. In addition, he developed a financial planning business to supplement his teaching salary and over time was able to build this business to one that brought in a sizable income. He even found himself needing to hire several employees to help him grow and build that planning business. In the end, Steve had the best of both worlds. Today, he teaches at the business school and operates a successful financial planning business on the side.

Endgame, or New Game?

Every end is a new beginning.

—Anonymous

It's commonplace these days to read in the newspaper or discover on social media that there's a universal trend toward postponing retirement. Some of the reasons are financial, but the reality is individuals are staying active longer. Further, exercising our brains through work can extend our lives and provide meaning in our later years. My view of retirement is this: **Don't do it!**

To my mind, retirement has many negative connotations. "She retired last year" all too often leads to "Oh well, I guess it's time for the senior center. Anyone up for a spirited game of hearts?" This is a direct path to emotional and mental breakdown. A recent report from the Employee Benefit Research Institute, which tracked retirement trends from 1998 to 2012, showed that the number of individuals who retired during these years and categorized themselves as "not at all satisfied" had steadily increased over this period of time.[2] Bottom line, the number of retirees who are not happy in retirement is increasing.

A better strategy—find your passion and put yourself to work doing it. I call this "re-directing." It does not need to be full-time, although it can be. Part-time work is an excellent way to redirect. Many of us have found ourselves in the uncomfortable position of figuring out what to do next. Individuals in their midfifties who've been forced out of their jobs, or even those individuals in their forties who have made enough money to live comfortably, must find direction in the second phase of their life to stay active, useful, and productive.

In my experience, I have seen countless success stories of individuals redirecting—rather than retiring—and in the process finding fulfillment and happiness.

JOHN, THE UNHAPPY, WELL-PAID
RESTAURANT EXECUTIVE

John was a successful restaurant executive who spent twenty-plus years in the restaurant business. Not that he liked it—in fact he hated the hours—but he liked the compensation and financial rewards.

He had worked for several national chains and relocated countless times to take on more senior-level positions. He made significant sacrifices during his career and was now at the top of his chosen field as the senior vice president in charge of restaurant operations for a major conglomerate. He had more than twenty restaurants under his management authority, all across the United States. Then one day at the age of forty-eight, he was out of a job. Game over. The firm was bought out, and his job was eliminated. He had relocated his family too many times and, with kids in high school, could not consider another move. What to do?

John focused on *Be, Know, Do*. He spent time thinking about what his skills were and how they might be applied to a cross section of industries. He then developed a list of possible industries where his skill set could be utilized. John had spent a great deal of time in a restaurant career, sourcing potential locations for expansion. This was an aspect of his career that he had really enjoyed. John first tried working as an executive for an extended stay–type hotel chain and found it was not a good fit. He went back to the drawing board and decided to pursue public storage business opportunities. This turned out to be a winner! He landed a job he loved, managing over ten properties, which played to his strengths and did not require relocation or the horrible hours associated with the restaurant business. Although John had been unwilling to leave the restaurant business and give up his lucrative pay and benefits, when he was forced out, he discovered he enjoyed each day more. In John's case, having passion for what he did brought him more satisfaction than being held hostage by a paycheck.

We all have the wherewithal to create opportunities in our lives, transform negative experiences into positive ones, and find our sweet spot of happiness.

Not everyone's "sweet spot" is entrepreneurial. There are also many corporate opportunities available when trying to redirect.

Job-Search Strategies

Results! Why, man, I have gotten a lot of results!
I know several thousand things that won't work.

—Thomas Edison, American inventor

Where to Look

Job searching is like a piñata—
if you hit it hard enough, you'll be rewarded.
—Anonymous

Over the years I have often been asked the question, "Where is the best place to look for a job?" That's difficult to answer, because in today's employment market there are so many different avenues to pursue—some better than others—and the options seem endless. Those new to the job-hunting process can find themselves overwhelmed with information, dos and don'ts, and so-called experts telling them what's right and what's wrong.

Truth be told, the absolute best source for potential employment opportunities is utilizing your own personal network of contacts. There is no better source! This form of networking produces the best results.

However, don't rely on only this one source. I always advise individuals to cast a very wide net and to develop and execute a multidimensional job search. The best results are obtained by having a multitude of search strategies, sources, and approaches. Having many different balls in the air will yield the best results.

The following list ranks my top ten best sources to consider as you begin your job search:

1. **Personal contacts:** The quickest way to find a job is through your own personal contacts. These are your A-list contacts—individuals you know and can personally reach out to for advice, direction, and job leads. Obviously the longer you've been working, the more your list of contacts will expand and increase; but even new college graduates know people. The list is not only professional contacts; it should also include family and friends. Use these contacts. This is not the time to be shy about working your contacts.

2. **Networking:** Your second best source is networking. Networking means using your existing contacts to get new contacts. It's meeting new people, participating in your professional association, attending conferences, and the like. Staying in touch with other professionals who can help expand your network, personal brand, and reach is paramount. (For more on networking, including how to make contacts, see pages 52–54.)

3. **Social media:** Today, social media is the lifeline to new jobs and job postings across every discipline imaginable. LinkedIn (the most popular business-oriented social network), Facebook, and Twitter all have job sites available to people looking for employment. Posting your resume on these sites can lead to very positive results, because many employers use these sites and other social media to source talent. (For more on this, see page 51.)

4. **Recruiters/Headhunters:** Another major source to consider is recruiters. Recruiters, often referred to as headhunters, can be a helpful resource for job seekers. Recruiters fall into two

categories: those working on a contingency, and those who will receive an up-front search retainer, which is directed to more senior professionals and often referred to as "retained search." Make sure you know the difference—and don't hesitate to ask. (See pages 80–81 for more details.)

5. **Job boards:** These sites are still valuable as sources, since many employers search for talent through job boards. Monster, CareerBuilder, and Glassdoor are online examples. They are all good sources. Another significant change taking place in this sector is the surge of "job aggregators" in the marketplace. These sites are powerful sources because they aggregate job listings from employer websites, publications, association websites, and other job boards into one central location. These job-search engines (aggregators) are massive and global. Websites like SimplyHired and Indeed.com are examples; they list positions by specific discipline, profession, experience, and geography. They also contain useful information about salary ranges and other helpful job-hunting details.

6. **Employer websites:** Going directly to specific employer websites is not a waste of time, as many might claim. Caution: Don't use this as your only source and method, because you could be stuck with a long and slow process! However, every major organization has invested money and time in creating career pages on their websites for the sole purpose of recruiting external hires. Don't underestimate the potential here.

7. **Classified ads:** It's hard to believe, but there are still organizations using online journals and printed magazines, such as

The Economist, The Wall Street Journal, and even local papers to recruit talent. Lower-level positions are often advertised on places like Craigslist. Smaller organizations use this as a low-cost solution to recruiting.

8. **Professional journals and associations:** These affiliations and publications will often have a career section with positions posted. For example, I'm a member of several professional organizations that do this. The International Coach Federation has a website with online job postings. Most professional associations have equivalent websites that can be excellent sources for job openings. The National Association of CPAs is one that comes to mind; you will find others as well.

9. **Alumni groups:** Another excellent source to use in finding positions is alumni associations. What better place to post jobs than your alma mater? Many academic institutions are famous for having broad and far-reaching alumni networks. For example, Harvard Business School is known to have such a network, as do many institutions across the country.

10. **Google:** Still the primary search engine for all job seekers, Google has excellent tools for individuals at all levels— whether they're looking for work or just wishing to explore career opportunities.

The best way to approach the job market and launch a career change is to use a combination of these ten sources. Job hunting is not an exact science; it's more of an art. Be prepared to mix things up a little.

THE IMPORTANCE OF BEING LINKEDIN

Social media avenues, like LinkedIn, have become a key source for job hunters to connect with professionals and search for new opportunities. Social media in business allows you to build a brand and expand your outreach. It can quickly allow you to develop a global network faster than you were ever able to do in the past. There is no doubt that these tools have revolutionized the job-search process. LinkedIn is the most commonly used, and currently has more than two hundred million members. Many Fortune 500 companies use it to source external talent.

For many job seekers today, LinkedIn is the first place to start the search. It begins with building a LinkedIn profile page. The advantage of the LinkedIn profile page is that it allows you to showcase yourself, much more than the traditional resume can. For example, the profile page gives you the ability to share videos, presentations, professional status updates, and even blog postings. This allows you to really create a "brand" for yourself and then to market that brand.

The second advantage of LinkedIn is that it offers users the ability to join industry groups, which allows you to network with thousands of contacts. I advise my career-coaching clients to join as many groups as possible, focusing in on those groups that are specific to their backgrounds and areas of professional interest. Joining groups for the sake of joining groups will not help you; be selective. Individuals can join up to fifty different groups on LinkedIn. Your individual electronic connections on LinkedIn are your modern-day version of your network.

Relationship Building— Code for Networking

It's not what you know, but who you know, that counts.

—Anonymous

How many times have you heard this cliché? We may not buy into it one hundred percent; but when it comes to career management, relationship building is extremely important! In today's world of social media, networking equals business success. There are many online tools at your fingertips, which can facilitate relationship building through networking. LinkedIn is best known for professional networking, and it has changed the landscape in terms of job hunting, networking, and advancing your career. Other social networking tools are also available for marketing yourself. These tools are essentially free and only require you to reach out, communicate, and sell yourself.

It does not matter what you do professionally; building a solid foundation of contacts is key to your success and development. Joining a professional organization, regularly attending seminars/conferences, and getting involved at those events will expand your network exponentially.

You are your own best marketing tool.

Who you socialize with, socially and professionally, can benefit your career. Accept invitations to participate within your professional association, run a project, participate on a panel, organize an evening event, etc. All of these things work to your advantage in building your network.

Nonprofit work is also an excellent way to build your network. If you don't already have one, find a cause or two you believe in—whether it's building schools in low-income neighborhoods or running a bake sale for the local animal shelter. Volunteer where you can. You may even serve on a nonprofit board. Get involved. It is good for you professionally, and good for your soul.

FROM SMALL NONPROFIT TO
A LARGE-SCALE CORPORATE FOUNDATION: LAUREN

Lauren was a successful fund-raiser and community advocate for a national nonprofit organization. As head of fundraising for this organization, she had achieved much success. She was talented, intelligent, outgoing, and driven. She had graduated at the top of her class from a prestigious university in Philadelphia, Pennsylvania. Her only issue, however, was compensation; pay levels in the nonprofit world pale in comparison to the for-profit world. Lauren set a goal for herself to try to parlay her experience in the nonprofit world to a similar role within a for-profit organization. The question was, how should she do that?

I met Lauren during my tenure as a board member for the nonprofit where Lauren was employed. Over the course of a year, we worked together on several fund-raising initiatives. I got to know Lauren as extremely capable. She eventually confided in me that she wanted to transition to general industry and was at a loss as to how to make this happen. Coincidentally, I happened to have a friend who was head of HR at a major energy services organization that had recently started a corporate foundation. This firm, a sizable publicly traded organization, was putting together an entire corporate initiative centered on their newly formed foundation. I spoke to Lauren about this and worked with her to help package her experience and qualifications. She put together a strategy paper on how she would take this organization's foundation and corporate initiative to the next level. I suggested she role-play her pitch with me to refine the material and her message.

I then introduced Lauren to my friend, the HR director. Lauren's passion, pitch, and personality won her the position. Today Lauren is the executive director for this organization's corporate foundation and global outreach. She has developed their overall program strategy and raised the profile of this foundation significantly.

Lauren was driven to succeed and used every opportunity to expand her qualifications. She enrolled in an executive MBA program and completed her degree through the company's tuition-reimbursement program. It is possible to put your passion to work for you, and Lauren's success offers proof.

Informational Interviews

Knowledge is power. Information is liberating.

—Kofi Annan, former secretary-general of the United Nations

Informational interviews are a key part of your research and networking. Originally introduced by Richard Bolles in his book *What Color Is Your Parachute?*, these types of interviews have become common practice for today's job seeker. An informational interview allows you to seek career advice from people already working in the field you wish to enter. Interviewing just for information, rather than for an actual job, will provide important data points that you can factor into either expanding your career search or narrowing it, depending on the outcome of the interview. Yes, this process can take time; but it has multiple benefits. First, you are getting in front of individuals that not only can provide valuable information but also may be able to refer you to a potential job opportunity they know about. Second, it gives you an opportunity to do some "practice" interviewing and to fine-tune your message and presentation.

How do you get in front of the "right" individuals to conduct this type of interview? Referrals are the best way. Family, friends, and former colleagues may be able to refer you to someone. This is the best place to start. A "soft" introduction from that individual via email is invaluable.

Researching target organizations and identifying someone within that target is another way. Today, LinkedIn is probably the best tool for doing this type of research. Cold calls to these individuals may have a low yield in terms of results, but if you get one interview that leads to the right career opportunity and position, it will have been worth the time.

A sample informational interview request letter (sent via email) is shown next.

SAMPLE EMAIL FOR SETTING UP
INFORMATIONAL INTERVIEW

Dear Jennifer Parker,
Matt Stone, a former colleague of yours, gave me your name and thought you would be a good contact for me to network

with. I have decided to pursue my career options and am now in the process of zeroing in on target opportunities.

After I graduated from Columbia, I joined a major Wall Street firm and spent three years in their investment banking analyst program. After completing my MBA at the University of Michigan, I joined a consumer products organization, where I worked in corporate strategic planning, reporting directly to the CFO.

I am now ready for a change and hope to transition back into financial services, where I can use my background in strategy, planning, and development. As you are currently in the Corporate Planning Office at **Company Name** throughout doing the type of work I'm interested in, I thought your advice, guidance, ideas, and suggestions would be helpful to me as I begin my search.

I look forward to new challenges and promising opportunities and would welcome the opportunity to speak with you. Would you be willing to talk with me about this? I will call your office next week to follow up, and if you have the time, I will schedule a convenient time for us to talk. As a reference, I have attached a copy of my resume.

Thank you in advance for your time.

Best regards,

Ted Smith

These types of interviews can be important in expanding your network and getting in front of decision makers who can help you in your job search. And remember, you should always follow up afterward with a thank-you note.

Several years ago, I was working with an individual who used the informational interview approach. In her case, the outcome was extremely positive.

INFORMATIONAL INTERVIEW
LANDS A JOB: SOPHIE

Sophie was a recent college graduate with a BBA degree in real estate. She wanted to get into commercial real estate development and was having a difficult time networking. With several summer internships working in property management on her resume, she had something to work with. One of the recommendations I made to Sophie was to go ahead and take her real estate licensing exam. She passed and was able to include that on her resume.

After retooling her resume and practicing her elevator speech and message, she was ready to start the informational interview process. A property manager she had interned with had a friend who was a senior partner for a major real estate firm. I suggested that she ask him whether he would make an introduction. After an email introduction, Sophie scheduled an appointment with this person to conduct her informational interview. To prepare her, she and I developed questions she would ask:

- "How did you get into this field?"
- "Does your firm offer any type of internship?"
- "In your role, what do you find frustrating?"
- "What are the competencies and attributes that you think are important for someone in your role?"

- "Can you suggest anyone else who might be a good source of information?"

Sophie had a very productive meeting. Several weeks later, this individual referred her to another organization that he knew was looking for a junior commercial real estate broker to help build their industrial development practice. Sophie interviewed for the position and was offered the job. Informational interviews do work.

Resume Upgrade

If you don't have a competitive advantage, don't compete.

—Jack Welch, former chairman and CEO of GE

I'm often asked whether a resume is needed in today's business landscape. After all, most open job postings are done online, where the applicants follow the online template to post their background. Is Google or LinkedIn the "new" resume? There is no denying that the Internet is an important tool to use in any job search and career transition, but the reality is that a well-thought-out and properly constructed resume is still needed, even in today's modern world of Twitter, Facebook, etc.

Your resume is a personal reflection of who you are and what you have accomplished, and as such, it is a key marketing tool. When it comes to resume preparation, opinions often vary: Should it be functional or chronological? Do you need a career summary? One page or two? It's enough to make your head hurt! There are as many ideas and views on how to construct a resume as there are colors in a rainbow. The truth is that resume preparation can take several different forms and still be acceptable—so long as it does its job.

Your resume must attract the attention of potential employers and provide a focal point of conversation during an interview. Based on my years of experience as a human resources executive and professional coach, here are some thoughts to consider:

- **Format:** Generally, the preferred format is the chronological resume. This style lists employment history in reverse order (newest first) and presents your background in a clear, straightforward manner. Alternatively, a functional resume will present more of a career summary and highlight those areas you want to emphasize. This resume style will stress the functions in which you have been involved and will downplay employment history. This format may be used if your employment history has been erratic. Most importantly, your resume should reflect your uniqueness as a candidate and your personal brand.

- **Length:** Simply put, a wordy resume will not be read. It is one of the first "knockout factors." A two-page resume is the acceptable length. Keep in mind that the length can vary based on your years of experience; a third page can be added. When it comes to resume length, remember to keep it brief, concise, and to the point.

- **Action words:** Your resume should include action words to describe your experience and background. Words such as "coordinated," "organized," "directed," and "accomplished" should be used. (See appendix B at the back of the book for a list of action words.) Tell the reader what you have done; don't just list job duties.

- **References:** References are an important part of the resume and employment process. Never, ever put the names and contact details of your references into the body of the resume. For one, it dilutes their value. At the end of your resume, type "References available upon request." References will fall into two categories: personal and professional. Your references are sacrosanct, in that they are yours and yours alone. Prior to giving out a reference, always give the person a courtesy heads-up that XYZ Company may call them.

In the end, a well-constructed resume will play a major role in getting you an interview. The rest is up to you. I have never met a resume that got hired; people get hired, and your resume must reflect your uniqueness as a person.

Target the Cover Letter

You can't judge a book by its cover.

—Anonymous

Cover letters are misunderstood and often seen as a resume substitute. In reality, they regularly contain too much information, they are often glossed over, or they are simply not read. As organizations have expanded their career sites, where recruiting is done via their online portal, cover letters are used less and less. It's important to note that when submitting your resume through an online portal, you'll need to include a job objective that closely mirrors the position for which you are applying.

Even in today's employment market, a well-constructed cover letter is important to have at your disposal to use at the right time. Whether used for networking, for making introductions, or for general marketing purposes, the cover letter is needed in your job-hunting toolbox.

The following letters are worth considering—one as an example of a poorly constructed cover letter, the other as that of a well-constructed cover letter.

PERSONAL LETTER
(INFORMING A PROSPECTIVE CONTACT OF YOUR INTENT; COULD BE USED AS PART OF YOUR CONTACT NETWORK)

[Company]
[Department]
[Ms./Mr.] [Name]
Dear _____ :

I have decided to pursue my career objectives elsewhere due to the relocation of the engineering division in which I'm currently working. My goal is to find a senior mechanical engineering or senior project engineering position.

I will be leaving my present position within the next few months and am now in the process of zeroing in on target organizations and search firms.

Enclosed (attached) is a copy of my resume to bring you up to date with my background, experience, and accomplishments and also to serve as a means of asking you for your advice, guidance, and suggestions. If you have a contact or know of any opportunities that fit my background and experience, please let me know. My contact details, including my email address, cell phone number, and LinkedIn profile link, are also included.

Sincerely,

LETTER OR EMAIL IN RESPONSE TO AN ADVERTISEMENT

[Company]
[Department]
[Ms./Mr.] [Name]
Dear _____ :

Your advertisement in the July 12 issue of *The Wall Street Journal* for chief financial officer caught my attention, and I would like to know more about the position.

As my enclosed (attached) resume indicates, I have fifteen years' experience in senior financial leadership positions, including the past ten years as the CFO for a major Fortune 500 manufacturing organization. My background has provided the level of organization exposure described in your ad. I have a master's degree in accounting and hold an active CPA designation.

I would appreciate an opportunity to discuss your needs and my background, and I look forward to your reply.

My contact details, including my email address, cell phone number, and LinkedIn profile link, are also included.

Sincerely,

SAMPLE NETWORKING EMAIL USING A SPECIFIC REFERRAL

Hi Jim Andrews,

My name is Carey Anderson—I was given your name by Scott Foster, a former colleague of yours, and I wanted to introduce myself. I hope this note finds you well.

I work at Bank of America and just returned to New York after living in Hong Kong for the past five years. I'm a senior human resources executive and have worked in financial services for seventeen years. While in Hong Kong, I was chief human resource officer for Asia Pacific and led a team of over one hundred HR employees across all human capital areas with a client base of over five thousand Asia Pac–based employees.

I'm in the process of exploring external employment opportunities. It would be great to have an introductory conversation at your convenience. Do you have time next week to connect? My office number is (212) 555-0166, or mobile is (212) 555-0166. My resume is also attached.

Many thanks—look forward to speaking with you soon.
Best,

SAMPLE OF A POORLY WRITTEN COVER LETTER

Dear _____ :

I am currently a master of business administration student at UCLA Anderson School of Management and will be graduating in June 2017. With prior experience in fixed-income trading and financial engineering, all in financial services, I believe I am an ideal candidate for an internship position with **Company Name**. The qualifications that I have, which make me a natural fit for an internship, include the following:

- A track record in the financial services industry with demonstrated accomplishments across a number of different roles within fixed-income trading
- Professional experience as a financial engineer supporting the fixed-income proprietary trading desk
- Exemplary communication skills, both written and verbal
- Exposure to working directly with clients on solving their technical issues and problems

- An academic background, which includes a bachelor's degree in finance and economics from the University of Pennsylvania
- A team player personality, strong competitive drive with the ability to perform under pressure

I have a passion for business and have proved that I have the right technical and interpersonal skills to work in a demanding work environment. I am convinced that I would be a good fit for your organization. In addition, having completed my first year's academics in the Berkeley MFE program will complement my background and make me an even stronger candidate for a position within your fixed-income trading division.

In conclusion, I have no doubt that I have the necessary skills, work experience, and personality to have an immediate impact on **Company Name**. I am ready to prove to you that I can be a valuable asset.

I have attached my resume for your reference and hope to speak with you soon.

Kind regards,

Issues with this letter: First, it's too long. It will never get read. Second, the tone of the letter is arrogant. This is not the way you want to present yourself to a prospective employer.

THE FOLLOWING SHOWS HOW
THE PREVIOUS LETTER SHOULD BE REWRITTEN

Dear _____ :

I am currently an MBA student at the Anderson School of Business, at UCLA, and will be graduating in June 2017. I would welcome the opportunity to be considered for an internship position with **Company Name**.

I have attached my resume for your reference about my background, experience, and accomplishments. As you can glean from my resume, I have substantial experience in fixed-income trading and financial engineering with several large financial institutions. I'm looking for a three-month summer internship position; I'm available to begin working on May 15.

I will follow up with your office in the next week in the hope we might be able to schedule an introductory phone conversation.

Thank you for your consideration.

Kind regards,

Etiquette

The world was my oyster, but I used the wrong fork.

—Oscar Wilde

When you think about job-search strategies, etiquette is often the last thing on your mind. But it should be at the top of the list! Over the course of my career, I have seen individuals make mistakes that I considered no-brainers or just lacking in common sense. Understanding simple acts of etiquette can be a game changer. Let's start with phone etiquette. It is critical to return phone calls ASAP, and definitely within twenty-four hours. As many people are extremely busy, if you do leave a voice mail, be sure to speak clearly, state the reason for the call, and leave your name and phone number—twice. For those with difficult or lengthy names, it is advisable to spell them out. Busy people do not listen to lengthy messages; they have a hair-trigger finger for the Delete button. Messages should be concise and to the point.

Regarding email communication, I consider it a very bad job-search practice when someone includes an emoji in his or her email communication. A smiley face at the end of your thank-you email is not a good practice and certainly not needed.

When you have a phone conversation, be sure not to dominate the conversation; instead, practice being an attentive listener. If and when you get an interview, arrive early and dress according to the organization's culture and the position for which you are interviewing. Occasionally, dress code etiquette is listed on the company's website, or you might glean this information from the informational interviews you previously conducted. Simple things regarding dress code are often overlooked, like men ensuring their shoes are clean and polished. You do not want to show up for an interview in leather shoes that look like you just pulled them from a backstreet dumpster. Also, in some corporate environments, the wearing of open-toed shoes by women can be frowned upon.

First Impressions

You never get a second chance to make a first impression.

—Harry Simmons, author of *Successful Sales Management*

I can't remember when I first heard this expression, but what a powerful message—particularly to those thinking about a job search or career change. First impressions are important! As you navigate the trials and tribulations of a long career, or prepare for that all-important job interview process, you want to avoid situations where you constantly second-guess the impression you made. In less than one minute, people will often form an impression of you. This is sad but true. So, what are those things you should be working on to ensure you make a lasting positive impression?

First, begin with how you present yourself. Posture, attire, eye contact, and a firm handshake are a start. You want to look and act polished and professional. In addition, listening and thinking before you speak are critical to a positive first impression. I'm a firm believer that we learn more by listening than we do by talking. A short pause before you answer a question is an excellent way to avoid saying something you will regret later.

Generally, when it comes to first impressions, it's easier to make a good one when you've had time to prepare. Thinking in advance about the questions you want to ask is critical. To improve, you can role-play and practice, which is where coaching can help.

However, in situations that are impromptu and sudden, you don't have time to prepare and often need to think quickly. That's where your "elevator speech" comes in. What is your elevator speech? In short, it's your professional statement—short enough to be shared during an elevator ride. The elevator speech should contain an introduction (including your name), who you are, your accomplishments, your background, and your objective for reaching out to the listener. Having your elevator speech ready at all times is key to making a good first impression. Professionals should be able to introduce themselves in a clear and concise manner. Rehearse it. Say it out loud to a third party to test your delivery. Have it ready so you are not caught flat-footed one day when you just happen to come upon the very person who might be able to give you, or direct you to, the perfect job.

Another type of elevator speech is being able to articulate

what projects you are involved in and to give a status update at a moment's notice. During my corporate tenure, I would always tell my staff to have their elevator speech ready at all times, because they could not know when they might bump into a manager and/ or senior leader who might ask for a quick update on a project they were working on.

My personal example of this? I was traveling to Germany to take part in a global conference where I was presenting on a specific topic. The CEO of my organization's parent company was going to be in attendance. I knew this person from prior meetings. During my layover in San Francisco, en route to Germany, I ran into the CEO, who just happened to be boarding the same flight. He was flying back to Germany, where he was based. Of course he asked me for a quick update on my topic and presentation. I had perhaps two minutes; thankfully, I was prepared. These kinds of interactions can be important to making a lasting impression. Never get caught off guard.

The Interview Process

Failing to prepare is preparing to fail.

—**John Wooden,** quoting a popular saying from his childhood

When it comes to interview preparation, no truer words have been spoken. John Wooden, the college basketball Hall of Fame coach, knew a few things about preparation! After all, he won ten NCAA division championships.

The job interview is the culmination of a great deal of planning, preparation, and marketing efforts. It is extremely important, therefore, that your first impression be positive. Let's face it; interviewing is stressful. However, with the right amount of thought and preparation, you can eliminate much of the stress and pressure.

During an interview, you are proving yourself on two levels. First, you are showing the potential employer that as a person, you are someone of character and integrity. Second, you are attempting to show you are the right person for the job, someone with the requisite skills and experience. This is a lot to accomplish during an interview!

John Lucht, in his book *Rites of Passage*, uses the analogy that when you are interviewing for a position, the employer is making a purchasing decision. You are the product, and the potential employer is deciding which product to buy. To take this thought a step further, you are not just the product; you are the salesperson as well. A very important part of the interview process is to sell yourself, to separate yourself from all others.

As you think about and prepare for an interview, start with the basics. Arrive on time. In fact, be early to get yourself ready. Dress appropriately for the organization you are interviewing with. Appearance and behavior are the first things to be noticed. The formal greeting, body language, and posture are all important things to think about as you start the interview. More importantly, always maintain eye contact with the interviewer. Throughout the interview cycle, maintain a positive frame of mind; go into every interview with the real desire to win.

All interviews effectively have a structure: beginning, middle, and end. Knowing this helps you manage the flow and ensure you have enough time to make your points. Job interviews are not the time to go into your life story with long autobiographical summaries. In advance, think about potential questions the employer may ask. Have your thoughts and answers prepared in advance.

This type of preparation will give you the right level of confidence you need to be successful. Research the company, review your qualifications, and be prepared for a series of interviews across the organization. Interviews will often begin with the human resources (HR) department; the larger the organization, the more formal the HR process. Operating group interviews conducted by the different line functions are also common today, with competency-based questions asked by the different interview teams.

Why all this preparation and planning? Today's world is highly competitive. You must be prepared to show how you differentiate yourself from other job prospects. With this preparation, you will show the employer that you are serious about what you are doing. During the early phase of the dot-com boom of the late 1990s and early 2000s, employers adopted casual dress as the new standard. I will never forget a comment from a CEO I worked with who said, "I will never be casual about my business, so I will never accept 'casual dress.'" Bottom line: Don't be casual about your interview preparation.

REBOUNDING FROM A FAILED INTERVIEW: MARIE

Marie was a seasoned professional with a master's degree in economics from a well-known school on the East Coast. Following her graduation, she joined a large financial institution in Boston, which she had previously interned with over two summers. She worked in their equity research department as a senior research analyst, covering a specific sector of the market. Unexpectedly, her husband was offered an opportunity with his firm to transfer to the West Coast to take on a management role. He accepted the transfer, and Marie was now in the job market for a new opportunity. A former client referred Marie to me; she was interested in some coaching for interview preparation. It had been almost ten years since she had done any interviewing, and Marie felt she needed some help as she began her job search.

We scheduled a number of sessions, where we worked on her interviewing skills. Shortly thereafter, Marie was a finalist for a position she desperately wanted. She thought this opportunity was the right position and right organization; although, they were looking for someone with a slightly different industry background from an equity research perspective. She wanted to branch out from her prior focus; that's what excited her about the role. Before her final day of interviews with this organization, we went through a role-playing session as if she were in an actual interview. I did not give her the list of interview questions in advance.

During her full day of interviews with the company, Marie did not do well. Even after all this preparation! It turned out the organization was really looking for someone with a different skill set, and her background and experience did not match up well with their expectations. Many of the technical questions they asked her were outside her scope of knowledge and expertise. Marie was heartsick over this considering all her preparation efforts. She felt like a failure, even though this outcome had nothing to do with Marie's competence, knowledge, or experience.

Several weeks later, another opportunity came up with another organization that was looking for someone with a background more in line with Marie's experience. She agreed to meet with the company. However, this time around was different. First, during a phone interview, she prequalified that her background was the right fit and compatible with their expectations. Second, she went into the final interview schedule relaxed, not focusing on the outcome, and just being herself. In addition, we did one last round of interview pretraining. She got the job.

Failure is never final; in reality, it's an opportunity to learn from the experience.

On the next pages you will find three areas related to job interviews. These are sample interview questions, questions related to your "management" style, and salary negotiation ideas.

SAMPLE INTERVIEW QUESTIONS

The following interview questions are the ones I think will, in one way or another, always come up during an interview. Keeping in mind that most interviews fall into well-defined segments, the following questions should be part of everyone's preparation.

Orientation segment

1. **Tell me about yourself.**

   Your response: Remember your elevator speech. No autobiographical narratives or life story!

2. **What are the words that best describe who you are?**

   Your response: Key in on three to four words that best describe you. Examples might be "ethical," "honest," "results oriented," and "problem solver." Be focused.

3. **What interests you in this position? How does your background and experience match up with the position?**

   Your response: Have a specific, well-thought-out answer that is tailored to the position for which you are interviewing. Again, keep your answer to two minutes or less.

4. **What do you know about our organization?**

   Your response: Know something about the organization:

what business the company is in; details regarding their management team, revenues, size, global footprint, and so forth. Again, keep your answer to two minutes or less.

Experience and achievement segment

1. **What are your short-term and long-terms goals?**
   Your response: In advance, write down three or four of them. Memorize them. Goals always come up during an interview. However, even if you're never given the opportunity to share them during the interview, your goal orientation will come through in everything you say.

2. **What are your top three achievements from your current position?**
   Your response: Be prepared to have specific achievements for each position you've held; have at least three for each position. Often interviewers will go through your background in chronological order asking specific questions about each position you have held. Be prepared.

3. **If you had to list one achievement that you felt helped define your working career, what would that achievement be?**
   Your response: This is the one question where it's time to brag a little. Think about the one theme that defines you. Being a consummate "team player" and having a continual focus on "process improvement" are examples.

4. **What are your primary strengths? How have they materialized and helped you in each of the positions you have held?**
   Your response: You should have your top three key strengths memorized. Be prepared to articulate how they have played out in each position you have held.

5. **What is your number-one weakness, and how have you overcome this during your working career?**

   Your response: We all have weaknesses, so be prepared to identify one that you can speak to. The right way to discuss a weakness is to think about how a weakness can also be viewed as a positive. For example, being a perfectionist can be a weakness, but it can also be seen as a positive in terms of your drive to do good work.

Introspective questions segment

1. **We have many qualified candidates to choose from for this position. Why should we hire you?**

   Your response: Here is another opportunity to shine a light on yourself! Have your answer planned out; role-play this with someone to practice the delivery. This is the type of question that allows you to really showcase your skills, experience, and talents.

2. **How do you perform under pressure?**

   Your response: The pat answer "When the going gets tough, the tough get going" is way too cutesy. On the one hand, many people cave under pressure, and you don't want to say that; but think through the right response. Having emotional intelligence is the ability to remain calm and level-headed during times of stress. Employers want to hear that you are self-aware and even-tempered while under stress.

3. **What is more important to you, money or personal satisfaction from the work you do?**

   Your response: The answer here really gets at your values. I always like to hear someone respond with the fact that they value the importance of money, and want to be paid fairly and consistent with their contribution, but that that's not what drives them to want to do better, improve, and add value. That satisfaction is what I call "psychic income."

4. **If I were to have a conversation with your current boss/supervisor, how would they describe you?**

   Your response: Think about the right approach to couch this response. It should mirror your strengths. Don't go over the top in using flowery language to explain this. Think about it from a serious perspective. What would your boss really say?

5. **What kind of constructive feedback have others given you regarding areas needing improvement?**

   Your response: The core issue to this question is the interpretation of how people view you, which may provide insights into your sensitivity, including how able and willing you are to accept negative feedback.

QUESTIONS RELATED TO MANAGEMENT STYLE

If you find yourself interviewing for a position involving managing or supervising other employees, you may be asked questions that probe your management style, your interpersonal skills, and your abilities to plan and make decisions. Here are some sample questions you should be prepared to address:

- Can you define your management style?
- Do you consider yourself a successful manager and supervisor? Why? Can you give examples?
- How many people did you hire in your previous position? How did you source the talent? What were the results (good and bad)?

- Have you ever had to terminate an employee? How did you handle this? What was your approach?
- What are your standards for performance? How would your employees describe them?
- How do you communicate, motivate, and develop staff?
- Describe your decision-making process.
- Can you give me an example of a really important decision you made in your previous position? Was it successful?
- Can you give me an example of a decision you made that backfired on you? What did you do to overcome this?

QUESTIONS RELATED TO SALARY EXPECTATIONS

Questions toward the end of the interview will often turn toward salary expectations. Salary requirements must be discussed; they're part of the negotiation process.

The number-one rule in this phase of the job search is— **don't negotiate against yourself**. Perhaps you've heard that you should "never be the first to mention a salary figure." This means you should always tell the employer that your salary expectations are negotiable and you are open to considering any reasonable offer they make. Don't get backed into a corner. The reality is that if you mention an incorrect figure, it *could* knock you out of the running. Every job needs to be looked at with both compensation and noncompensation factors in mind. Those nonsalary items include fringe benefits, working hours, the team you would work with, location of the employer, and others.

A word of caution: Online applications often ask you to name your target salary. Never put down a figure. Just insert "negotiable."

Practice, Role-Play, Research

For the things we have to learn
before we can do, we learn by doing.

—Aristotle, Greek philosopher

Just like actors who role-play as part of their professional training to learn their craft, we need to role-play the interview process. The best way to sharpen your interviewing skills is to practice interviewing. Even seasoned and experienced professionals need to refresh their skills. In my coaching practice, I have worked with professionals who have more than fifteen years' work experience—even they need help mastering the interview process. Anticipating the interview questions that might be asked is the best place to start, as well as establishing a congenial rapport from the outset. However, keep in mind it's important to let the interviewer control the flow. All interviews have a natural flow and follow some pattern, depending on whether it's your first, second, or third interview with a given employer.

The early orientation portion of the interview is the "let's get to know you" segment. The inevitable "tell me about yourself" question will be posed to you. Keep your answer short, two minutes or less. Employers are not looking for your life story! Your ability to put your answers into capsule-styled answers is very important. Exploratory questions will be asked about your work experience, education, career goals, and readiness. In addition, cognitive questions focused on your knowledge and technical expertise will be a focal point. In today's world we are seeing group interviews used more and more, centered on cognitive questions and problem solving, testing your intellectual capability. The high-tech industry (for example, Google) is known for this interview style.

Be prepared to discuss key segments of your experience and achievements. Have at your fingertips the ability to articulate three to five achievements for each position you have held during your career. Of course, questions regarding your strengths and weaknesses will come up. Be prepared to handle the tough questions, like your reasons for leaving all past employers. Most importantly, be prepared to discuss why you are interested in the organization and what appeals to you about the position. Know something about the organization—what makes them different from their competitors, what plans they have in the works, their strengths and weaknesses. Do the research. Search their website.

Be prepared to articulate how your background and experience fit the role for which they're hiring. To do these things effectively, you must research the organization and reread the position specifications to determine how your background lines up.

It's important to practice making a great impression that will position you ahead of the competition. What's the best way to do that? **Practice!**

Follow Up and Follow Through

There's clearly something to be said for success
and following through on your commitments.

—Frank Carlucci, former US secretary of defense

I have seen individuals make some fatal mistakes when it comes to follow-up and, more importantly, follow-through—for example, not sending a thank-you email after an interview. Simple and easy, right? I recall an instance when a leading candidate for a position did not send a follow-up note for more than a week. In this case, the hiring manager was a bit old-school; he did not hire that person. He felt it showed lack of interest, appreciation, and follow-through.

Another note of caution: If you interview with multiple individuals, don't send the same thank-you note, word for word, to each person. That would send the message "I'm too lazy to write individualized notes." Also, knowing that there may be multiple rounds of interviews, send a thank-you email after each interview cycle.

If you interview for that job of a lifetime—the position you really, really want—sending both a thank-you email and a handwritten note can add a winning personal touch.

Another important strategy to adopt is follow-through. For example, in the course of a long job search you will encounter many contacts through your networking activities. For those individuals who went out of their way to be helpful, make sure you continue to update them on your search progress. Once you land your new position, drop them a line to let them know. Better yet, send them a LinkedIn mail, because you should already be connected to them on LinkedIn at this point.

Dealing with Recruiters

Knowledge is power.

—**Francis Bacon,** English philosopher and author

The recruiting industry is often a hidden and mysterious one, filled with contradictions. First, it helps to understand what you are dealing with. Recruiters—or headhunters, as they are often called—fall into two distinct categories: contingency and retained. The primary difference between the two is how they operate and how they are paid. *Contingency* recruiters get paid for successful placement of their candidates—if their candidate gets hired. *Retained* recruiters are employed by the organization to do a specific recruiting assignment. They are paid a search fee up front (or over a span of time), regardless of whether anyone is hired. Retained search consultants are more consultative and work closely with the hiring organization to determine not only a candidate's technical fit from an experience perspective but also their cultural fit. There are a number of variations to this model, but generally the search industry falls into these two categories.

In terms of how recruiters operate, contingency recruiters have a tendency to send your resume out to as many potential employers as possible, in the hope that someone will express an interest. I call this the "flypaper" approach: send it out to as many targets as possible and hope it sticks somewhere. Their business incentive is based on volume. The potential problem with this approach is that you, the candidate, can lose control over the process and risk confidentiality being compromised. You don't want someone randomly sending your information to just any employer, so it's important to make that point up front with the individual recruiter.

Retained recruiters will often tell you they are working on a "confidential" search and can't reveal the client's name, thus playing a game of mystery with you. Don't fall prey to this tactic. You don't want to give them your resume unless you know where it's going and whether you are interested in the opportunity. The point here is not to blindly accept everything you are told. You should remain in control of your job search.

Keep in mind that recruiters can be very helpful in your job search. They can expand your network and introduce you to interesting opportunities. Just remember to ask the right questions so that you'll be in a position of knowledge and control in dealing with them.

One of the best sources of information on the recruiting industry is the Association of Executive Search Consultants (AESC), the trade association of professionally recognized recruiters. To be sure the recruiting firm you are dealing with operates with the highest ethical standards, inquire as to their membership.

Workplace Strategies

Man was born free,
and he is everywhere in chains.

—Jean-Jacques Rousseau, French philosopher

Happiness at Work—a Possibility?

Happiness is the valuable commodity,
and that's what makes life good.

—Neil Young, Canadian singer-songwriter and musician

As a fan of Neil Young, I was interested in an interview about his recently published memoir. In addition to being a songwriter and musician, he is a "motor head" and has owned hundreds of cars over his lifetime. In the interview, Young pointed out that at this stage of his life, he is focused on doing things that make him happy, including writing a book about his love of cars. As I pondered this, I began to think about happiness at work. How many of us are truly happy at work?

Are you just satisfied or are you "engaged"? There is a great deal of research on the issue of what motivates us to get up in the morning and go to work day in and day out. Employee engagement has recently become a focus of many organizations, particularly as they try to create a positive work environment, one that appeals to the millennial generation. A recent Gallup poll found that just twenty-nine percent of millennial workers were engaged in their jobs[1]— thus the reason for the focus on engagement. Are employees really happy at work? How do you really measure engagement?

"Engaged" employees feel passionately about their jobs and share their organization's values. Some employers use self-reporting surveys to attempt to measure employee engagement, while others look at specific behaviors that show commitment, drive, dedication, and social integration. But being satisfied at work is not the same as being engaged. Here's my simplistic example: Imagine you go on vacation and try a new restaurant. The food is good; the place had a pleasant atmosphere, the service is good, etc. You leave satisfied. Will you tell others about the experience? Probably not. However, during the same vacation you go to a different restaurant and have one of the best dining experiences of your life, one that is so terrific you simply can't stop talking about the experience. You tell all your friends about this restaurant experience: the food, the service, the wine list, the ambience, and so on. That's the difference in being just satisfied versus being engaged.

Employee engagement surveys will often attempt to measure the level of employee engagement versus employee satisfaction. Employees working just for the money are generally not engaged at work. They don't necessarily consider the psychic benefits of working; for them, the emotional and psychological rewards are secondary to the financial aspects of work. Plain and simple, they work to get a paycheck and support themselves. They may be one hundred percent satisfied, but not engaged.

A steady paycheck is important. But, over time, there is more to working than just receiving a paycheck. The intrinsic benefits of working are equally as important, if not more important, as the money we receive. This "psychic income" is critical to happiness at work. In my definition of psychic income, I include positive work relationships and personal satisfaction in your work. In his memoir, Neil Young describes happiness as "the valuable commodity," and in my opinion, happiness cannot be measured purely in financial terms. It is hard to find true happiness in money, and that's where fulfillment in our work comes into play. The short-term benefits of a paycheck are unquestionably important. However, over time the intrinsic or psychic benefits will outweigh any focus on money. We all want to get more out of working. In my view, over the long term, personal satisfaction—and more specifically "engagement"—is critical to happiness at work.

One of the most successful organizations in recent memory is Starbucks. Howard Schultz, CEO of Starbucks, has created a business model in which getting a cup of coffee is an "experience." I have been told that his senior managers running his operation don't leave. He has created a culture of engagement. Schultz has been quoted as saying, "Work should be personal. For all of us. Not just for the artist and entrepreneur. Work should have meaning for the accountant, the construction worker, the technologist, the manager, and the clerk."[2] That is the best definition of employee engagement that I can think of.

Monday Morning Horrors

*Choose a job you love, and you will
never have to work a day in your life.*

—Anonymous

I'm sure everyone has heard some version of this quote. Do you find yourself dreading Monday morning? For many of us, the beginning of the week is often the worst day of the week. Why is that? Is the monotony of a dead-end job acceptable because the thought of having to start over is far worse than the alternative? Often, because of our hectic lives and busy schedules, we are reluctant to take action and make a change. Each Sunday night, we mentally prepare ourselves to tackle the same increasingly empty role. Is it time to do something about those Monday morning horrors? You can begin by taking ownership, deciding what you love to do and want to do, and making a plan to find a position that accommodates your skills, talents, and passion.

Some caution is needed here; it is very important to have realistic expectations about doing what you love. We all have different passions. For example, I love music and have some talent as a guitar player. However, that does not mean I can make a living as a musician. We need to remember that we all have competencies, talents, and skills in certain areas. It's much better to have a realistic awareness of what you can and can't do. That being said, we can still change the way we approach our Monday mornings.

Whether it's the job, organization, or career choice you made, taking ownership and considering what, and how, you need to change is important. At times, the best medicine is a new position, or a change in environment to recharge your batteries. Other times, it's making small changes to your routine and approach to improve your current situation.

Regardless, taking specific action steps to change is the place to start. For example, if your boss is someone you just can't seem to get along with and you struggle to communicate with, that can make Monday mornings seem impossible. Making a few tweaks to your routine might help you with the "Monday morning blues." Consider tweaks such as these:

- **Plan ahead.** On Sunday night, think about the days ahead. What needs to be done in the coming week? What meetings, projects, and deadlines are coming up? Take a few minutes to think about these activities, or better yet, make a priority list, which will get you ready to face the week ahead with less stress.

- **Arrive early.** On Monday mornings, start getting in early. Why? Getting to work early allows you to have time to focus without interruption, possibly looking at your action list from the night before, checking emails, etc. This will allow you to start the week off on a positive note, in the right mental frame of mind.

- **Focus.** Instead of focusing on all the negatives aspects of your situation, focus on what needs to be done rather than what stresses you.

- **Improve performance.** It's always helpful to focus on improving your personal performance. It's hard to ignore top-tier performance. This may improve the communications issues with the boss. You might also consider seeking out a coach to help you communicate better with your boss. Small action steps will empower you.

What Is Your Strategy?

Have a vision, get a plan, and stay the course.

—Frederic Hudson, *LifeLaunch*

As professionals, we devote time and attention to what matters and to those activities that will get us to where we want to go. Do you have a career strategy, a workplace strategy, or, better yet, a "life" strategy? By life strategy I mean an all-encompassing plan that includes not only career plans but also life and personal goals, and includes asking questions such as where you want to live and whether you want to get married, have a family, and establish roots near your extended family.

When you sit down and think about it, where do you allocate your time, resources, and emotional energy? These are questions you should be contemplating as you develop career and workplace strategies. Most of us don't graduate from college knowing with certainty what we want to do. As we navigate the ups and downs of our careers, we normally find our way into something we enjoy doing . . . most of the time, anyway.

How Will You Measure Your Life? by Clayton Christensen and others is an excellent book, worth taking the time to explore. As a Harvard Business School professor, Christensen tracked the career paths of Harvard MBAs; and despite their professional accomplishments after graduation, many of them report being unhappy with their career choices. Hard to imagine, right?

Sometimes it takes many years to find our way in life, but it does not need to be that way. In my view, it comes down to an individual's makeup, or DNA. Some of us have a high need for achievement, status, success, and wealth. Others of us seek personal fulfillment through hobbies, our families, and personal interests. Regardless, we all are wired in certain ways that drive and motivate us to do what we do. Coming to terms with that reality is how our life strategy begins. For many of us, finding our personal passion, setting personal goals, finding the right career choice or right job, etc., comes easily. For others, it can take time—perhaps years—to realize. And that is okay as well. The important thing is to find what we love and then do it.

One of the tools I use in my coaching practice is the Hogan Motive, Values, Preferences Inventory (MVPI), which measures your motives, values, and preferences. Based on forty years of predictive analytics, this psychometric tool is an excellent way to measure one's internal makeup. I like it because it measures and shows what we really want, **not just what we say we want**. Do you value recognition, power, money, social status, or altruism? Gaining an understanding of these values and preferences is the start of taking control of your career and life and, ultimately, the start of guiding your strategy.

Having Passion

To be passionate is to be alive.

—**Jason Gay,** author and journalist

I love this quote from Jason Gay, *Wall Street Journal* columnist. He frequently writes on sports and social issues. One topic he writes about often is running. As a runner myself, I find that his columns on the topic always hit a nerve with me. Runners, and all athletes for that matter, have passion about what they do. Passion is also an important quality for business success. I believe it goes hand in hand with several key strategies to building and maintaining a successful career. Again, it does not matter what you do for a living; these three strategies will help you maintain the right attitude for success, both on the job and off:

- First, **have some passion for what you do**. It starts there. We spend most of our life working. In order to maintain the necessary work ethic, drive, and sustainability to make it, passion is a requirement. Without passion, you are racing toward extinction. Moreover, lacking passion in the workplace will automatically place you behind on the performance curve. Employees lacking passion fall into what I call the "plotter" category, those people who just show up day in and day out without drive or mission.

- Second, **you must constantly focus on self-improvement**. You should never be satisfied with yesterday's success. There is nothing wrong with taking a bow for today's accomplishments. A victory lap is okay—in fact, it can be important. Enjoy the moment, but always think of ways to improve and do better. This will lead to the right result.

- Last, **think like an owner**. What does that mean? In today's competitive world, owners must put clients first— put customers and products first to build a successful business. As you begin to think like an owner, it will lead to a significant change in your mindset. Thinking like the CEO of your own business changes the way you do things. It drives you to think in terms of excellence in all that you do. Moreover, it will guide you on how to spend the company's money and allocate resources.

These three simple rules for developing and maintaining passion will help you manage on a day-to-day basis and build a lasting career. As Jim Collins points out in his book *Good to Great*, we do not get from good to great by focusing on just average. To get beyond just average, you must have passion.

WHEN YOUR PASSION BECOMES YOUR JOB: JOAN

Joan was a successful technology executive. She had worked in a number of organizations and had difficulty finding the right fit. After college she somewhat stumbled into her technology career but never really enjoyed the work. After fifteen years in different technology roles, she was laid off when the company she was working for closed its US operation.

Joan had always been an active runner and in fact had completed a dozen marathons. She used running as a way to destress. It cleared her mind and gave her much fulfillment. She had also been involved with a nonprofit, helping to raise money by acting as a running coach for the marathon team. It turns out, this nonprofit had just received approval to hire a full-time paid staff member to run their athletic fund-raising efforts. This happened at the same time Joan was in transition. She took the job and found herself feeling much happier, and later also became a part-time running coach for the local high school cross-country team.

Personality and Organizational Fit

What matters most is not "what" you are but "who" you are.

—**DaShanne Stokes,** author of *The Unfinished Dream*

Personality plays a significant part in success or failure on the job. One of the paradoxes of being human is that we have different sides to our personality. The ancient philosophers describe this as the paradox between good and evil.

Personality plays a huge role in personal development. In my coaching, another Hogan tool I use is the Hogan Personality Inventory (HPI). This psychometric assessment helps individuals better understand their own personality, particularly their individual strengths and weaknesses. The Hogan assessment breaks down personality into two separate components, the "dark" side and "bright" side. The bright side of personality includes those personality characteristics considered strengths—tendencies that appear when we are at our best. The dark side of personality includes those characteristics that can cause us to derail and thereby underperform. These are tendencies that show up when we are at our worst.

During my career, I have seen many situations in which individuals with unlimited potential derail themselves because of their dark-side personality quirks. Bottom line, this is about how we are internally wired. It's important to understand how you are wired if you are to make the best career choice for yourself and, most importantly, determine the type of organization that fits your personality.

For example, some organizations are very structured, hierarchical, and process oriented. If you are more entrepreneurial and like a fast-paced, results-oriented culture, that type of organization would not be the best place for you to work. A recent coaching client of mine was an actuarial accountant by training, and he'd worked for many years with insurance organizations. His personality was very black and white; he liked structure, process, and routine. He had recently accepted a new role in risk management with a smaller start-up organization, one that was unstructured and entrepreneurial. This was a bad fit for him; he struggled in this environment, because it didn't fit his personality profile. He resigned after one year.

A person's "fit" within a job or organization will largely determine their success or failure. Research shows that seven in ten new hires derail in the first year of employment because of bad fit.[3] This is something to think about as you choose the right organization for you.

Thinking about fit **before** you accept a new role will help facilitate your success within the new organization and reduce your risk of derailing.

College Graduates

I want to say one word… Plastics!

—*The Graduate*

Every spring across the country we see thousands of "freshly minted graduates" ready to set the world on fire. Back in 1967, according to the film *The Graduate*, there was a future in "plastics." Prosperity was just around the corner, or so it seemed. How things have changed! Today there is no clear path to prosperity, unless you are a trust-fund baby, and even then, I'm not sure that's so clear. The current market is very competitive for entry-level employees, and college graduates face significant challenges in the competitive marketplace.

Not long ago I gave a presentation to the financial engineering graduating class at the University of California–Berkeley's Haas School of Business. I began my presentation by pointing out that the competition is tougher today than it ever has been, and the job-search process is more mentally challenging and demanding. According to a 2011 survey from the National Association of Colleges and Employers, for every one open position for new graduates, there was an average of twenty-one job applicants.[4] To be successful today requires not only competence and confidence; you must also be mentally tough and self-aware. Securing a new position today requires detailed career planning and execution.

Many of today's graduates are not properly prepared to face the real world. Also, many do not have a clear picture of what professional endeavor to pursue. In my mind, the key to success for new graduates is to be open to all possibilities. The traditional career path is no longer the only way to make an impact and find fulfillment. Regardless of what they do, new graduates need to be creative, flexible, inventive, and entrepreneurial.

Break the traditional rules once in a while; it could lead to interesting possibilities and opportunities. College graduates must expect the unexpected and be prepared for uncharted waters. Opportunities within the traditional corporate world will always be there; however, an increasing number of nontraditional careers and opportunities will become more commonplace in today's employment environment.

A recent survey conducted by leading labor economists Larry Katz and Alan Krueger pointed out that fifteen percent of individuals in the labor force today are working in some form of alternative work arrangements.[5] These mini-careers, so to speak, would be positions like independent contractors, temporary help agency workers, freelance consultants, and/or individuals holding multiple part-time positions. I found this to be interesting research into the future of the employment market and eye opening for college graduates.

Are We Really Listening?

Listen more than you talk.

Nobody learned anything by hearing themselves speak.

—Sir Richard Branson, founder of Virgin Group

For years during my corporate career, I frequently heard the statement "My boss just doesn't listen to me." Refusing to listen is an art form for many; they either lack the skills required to be a good listener or simply don't care. Regardless, most people are not very good listeners. I have always held the view that you learn more by listening than you do by talking. What a novel concept, right? What does it mean to be a really good listener?

One of my favorite books on this topic is *Co-Active Coaching*, which discusses listening in some detail and defines listening in terms of several levels. They describe the basic level of listening as one in which "our awareness is on ourselves."[6] In this type of listening, the focus is "me" centered. For example, getting directions to the nearest Starbucks . . . turn left at the stop sign, go three blocks, and make a right at the gas station, and it will be on your left in the middle of the block. Your focus is on hearing and receiving these directions while possibly asking yourself a series of questions: Is it going to take me a long time to get there? Am I going to have enough time to make it to my next appointment? (And so on.) Your focus is on "What does this mean to me?"—not on giving the other person any information. The highest form of listening is two-way communication, focused on that person and the conversation, in which you are gathering information with all your senses. This is what you hope for when you are having serious conversations on the job. This is real communication and the highest level of listening. Unfortunately, workplace conversations are often one sided—in which someone is barking out information.

We often hear about the concept of "active" listening, which is when you repeat back to the person with whom you are speaking what you heard them say. This technique would have you respond, "What I heard you tell me is . . ." You're clarifying what you've heard. This form of listening can be very effective in communicating with your boss and/or senior leaders. Active listening can be extremely helpful as you set up project details, due dates, and deadlines with your boss.

Conversations that don't include both people are counterproductive and can leave one person feeling like they were not heard or listened to. These conversations and this interplay on the job leave you frustrated. We have all had the dreaded performance review in which the person giving the review was not listening and didn't even seem to be in the same room with you. In my work with organizations on performance management training, I stress the importance of planning ahead to eliminate this all-too-common situation. Managers have an obligation to their employees to come prepared for a meaningful conversation, one in which listening is paramount. Real communication starts with good listening. This level of listening takes patience and practice—and we all need more practice. A helpful exercise is to start observing yourself to gauge how well you listen now. Solicit feedback from those around you—a spouse, a colleague, a friend, a mentor, and so on.

There are some lessons to be learned here, not only to become better listeners on the job but also to become better listeners in general. Our relationships will improve immensely.

A Dog's Perspective

The dog, as we've seen,
is a master looker, a skilled user of attention.

—Alex Horowitz, *Inside of a Dog*

I was recently out walking my dog, Maddie, when I realized we could learn some important lessons from dogs about effective workplace behavior. I'll admit it, I'm a dog person—always have been. Compared to humans, a dog's cognitive capability is extremely limited. However, we can learn a lot from our four-legged friends.

Admittedly, I'm not an expert in the psychology of dogs, but I do know one thing: dogs are *present.* Dogs live in the *now.* Dogs are not worried about what the future holds. Similarly, we need to master the skill of being present, thinking about what's going on now and not worrying about what happens in the future. When dogs want something, they are very attentive and will stare you down. In your daily workplace conversations with coworkers, on a job interview, or in interfacing with your boss, eye contact is very important. Part of being present is being attentive; it begins with eye contact. Years ago, I worked with someone who had the annoying habit of checking email every time he took a phone call. He was not very attentive, to say the least. All the successful leaders I have worked with were attentive; they were present, and they were good listeners.

What about body language? Dogs communicate with their tails, ears, and even their posture. Our body language can also communicate messages, both positive and negative. Our body language in any human interaction communicates important messages to the other party. Are we engaged? Do you appear to be somewhere else and totally removed from the conversation? Think about it the next time you have a workplace interaction. Were you attentive? Did your posture suggest something positive, or negative? Whether we realize it, we communicate through our movements—how you sit in a meeting, how you react to a colleague's point that may differ from yours. All of these movements matter.

Flexing to the moment is also an important skill to think about. To flex is to adapt your operating style to a given situation. At the workplace, our interactions fall within three basic categories: coworker to coworker, subordinate to boss, and boss to subordinate. It is advisable to adjust—flex—your responses, depending on which of these categories you find yourself in. You need to be willing to challenge others but also know when to back off. Everyone's communication style should be clear, professional, and respectful. I often see individuals in my coaching practice hold themselves back as a result of poor communication skills. Acknowledging where you have issues and taking the time needed to improve them will assist you in your success on the job.

In the end, it comes down to using effective and positive interpersonal skills. Without these, success on the job will be difficult and challenging.

Social Media and the Workplace

Distracted from distraction by distraction.

—T. S. Eliot, noted poet

Have you ever felt that the distraction caused by social media has taken us to new levels of disconnect? Today we are the victims of information overload. It seems that the only topic of conversation is "What's trending?" Between Twitter, Facebook, Instagram, Snapchat, LinkedIn, and others, we are inundated with information.

There is an additional downside to all of this, because these tools can have negative consequences if misused. Anything posted on a social media website is traceable and there for the world to see. There is no confidentiality of information.

What you do in your private life is no longer private once it is posted on social media. It can harm your reputation. It can cause an employer to discipline or dismiss an employee, like the recent incident in which a Taco Bell executive was caught on camera attacking an Uber driver and subsequently dismissed. It may also limit your job opportunities. Recently a coaching client of mine was offered a senior position with a large financial institution and was surprised to find out that part of the preemployment background check included a social media check, in addition to the standard criminal, credit, and other background checks. Remember, organizations are paying attention to how new employees use social media.

There are numerous websites where employees can post their grievances. One of the most popular is Glassdoor, where users post all types of information, including company reviews, interviewing experience, salary levels, and the like. The information posted is supposed to remain anonymous, but if you are accessing these websites from your organization's computer, it is traceable and leaves a permanent digital footprint. My number-one rule for using any social media outlet is this: Never, ever access these sites from your employer's computer, and don't post any comments regarding your company or colleagues. Lastly, don't allow the lines between your business life and personal life to become blurred. For example, accessing a dating website from your workplace computer is likely to get you fired. It's simply not smart. The perils of social media in the workplace are vast; use social media wisely.

It's extremely important to learn how to effectively use these tools to your advantage to maximize your career and personal goals.

Cell Phone Captive

My life is now a constant assessment of whether what's happening in real life is more entertaining than what's happening on my phone.

—**Damien Fahey,** writer for *Family Guy*

I was recently out having dinner with my wife and could not help but notice the couple next to us. They had their cell phones neatly placed on the table and the entire evening could not stop checking them. Sad but true. Have you ever felt you were tethered to your BlackBerry or iPhone? Or had the feeling you were a captive to the cell phone, not wanting to be away from any action at work, at the office, or in the latest incoming email? As a result, we can find ourselves cut off from the rest of the world.

In today's competitive business environment, we are expected to respond to emails as they come in. I get that. We have the responsibility to serve the needs of clients and ought to respond to internal issues that come up during the day. Moreover, reaction time in business is critical and often does separate excellent performance from average performance. Having a sense of urgency is important to maintaining high standards of performance. However, there is a balance in all of this.

At what point have we gone too far in never putting the Black-Berry away for a few minutes to just enjoy the moment and forget about work? Allowing our connection to work through our cell phones to take precedence over relationships, both business and personal, is going too far. The work will always be there; it does not go away. But relationships are harder to build; don't forget to take time away from busy work issues to "be a friend."

Do You Have Presence?

Presence is a state of awareness.

—**Doug Silsbee,** *Presence-Based Coaching*

When you think about our everyday interactions, the importance of presence cannot be overlooked. Presence is everything; it doesn't matter whether your interactions are social or professional. So, what is presence? Presence is being in the moment with the person with whom you are speaking. It shows caring, attention, and respect. A good listener is someone with presence, but it's more than just listening. It is also showing warmth and genuineness, not being distracted when interacting with someone. Why is this important? A lack of personal presence can derail you as you progress in your career.

Have you ever had the experience of your manager taking a phone call during your annual performance review? That is not being present! It's the antithesis of presence. Former president Bill Clinton had presence. Regardless of your political views, in his prime, he was the best at making people feel welcome.

How do you acquire presence? Just like any learned skill, you need to develop presence through practice. Most of us have either worked for someone or observed business leaders we admired because of their ability to be present, authentic, and attentive. Think about a recent interaction you had on the job with a colleague. Were you demonstrating presence? Were you paying attention, listening, and being mentally in the moment? If not, try it next time. You will find it can improve your work performance in terms of your interpersonal interactions. Moreover, it will help you build better relationships.

Every time you have a workplace interaction with someone, you have an opportunity to build a relationship. All interactions generally involve two things: First, there is the topic to be discussed or task to get done. Second, there is the opportunity to advance the relationship. Your presence and approach here is the opportunity to have a positive interaction and conclusion, a neutral one, or a negative one. These interactions are critical to building your professional reputation.

One of the most memorable experiences I had in my career at seeing real presence in action was years ago when I lived in Japan. I was part of a global cost-cutting initiative, which included significantly reducing the international allowances (housing, overseas premium, cost of living, etc.) of some seventy expatriates living and working in Japan and Asia. This was hitting these individuals right in the pocketbook. During the meeting announcing these changes, the CEO managing the business at the time wanted to conduct the meeting. He was walking right into the proverbial "buzz saw." He started the meeting and immediately turned it into a "good news" meeting. Yes, he was a good salesman, but his state of awareness and authentic style of communicating was "presence" at its best.

Inside/Outside

What lies behind us and what lies before us
are tiny matters compared to what lies within us.

—Henry Stanley Haskins, Wall Street trader

One of my favorite singer-songwriters is Keb' Mo'. I'm always inspired by his powerful lyrics. His song "Inside Outside" has some interesting implications for us as professionals. The theme of his song is that however we exist on the inside, we are also that way on the outside. Another way to think about it: Our thoughts on the inside influence how we interact with others (e.g., boss, peer, subordinate, client, customer, and so on). Negative or angry thoughts yield bad results. At times the ordinary difficulties of life in general are stressful. A slight shift in our perspective can be the best thing for us to get out of a rut.

If you find yourself thinking negatively about your specific situation, perhaps it's time to change your thoughts—change the way you think about it. Someone once told me that they hated their job so much, they would recite to themselves every night before falling asleep "At least when I sleep, the pain will go away." Very sad—that clearly is a negative frame of reference.

During your daily workplace interactions, negative thoughts will create a barrier to getting things done. Yes, at times we encounter challenges at work; dealing with difficult colleagues, office politics, and various other business pressures can be challenging. A constant focus on the negative can lead to a spiral of defeat and, over time, even depression.

In the book *Change Your Thoughts—Change Your Life*, Wayne Dyer uses the wisdom of the *Tao Te Ching* to teach us how to help shape our thoughts about life's difficulties. No matter what method you use—music, Chinese philosophy, whatever—thinking positively about a work problem is the first step in turning the situation around. Talking with a colleague, friend, or mentor about your feelings will also take the load off. I do believe we create our own reality; negative thoughts about your job, boss, or crummy salary will lead to negative consequences. On the flip side, positive thoughts create positive results.

Workplace Habits

We first make our habits, and then our habits make us.

—Doug Silsbee, *Presence-Based Coaching*

Habits have an interesting way of influencing our behavior, both on the job and away from work. Some are good habits, while others are bad. At times, bad habits can affect our professional life in very negative ways. Exactly what is a habit? A habit is anything we naturally do without consciously thinking about it. It's something you do on a regular basis. Doug Silsbee, author of *Presence-Based Coaching*, describes habits as being hardwired into our brain. Merriam-Webster defines *habit* as "a behavior pattern acquired by frequent repetition"—a thing done often and, hence, done easily.

Throughout our childhood we develop our habits. The way you hold your knife and fork when you eat is a habit. Most of us are essentially on autopilot when we wake in the morning and reach for the toothbrush to brush our teeth. Brushing your teeth is considered a good habit, unless you live in drought-stricken Southern California and leave the water running the whole time you're brushing. That would be a bad habit. Another bad habit might be constantly interrupting or finishing people's sentences. A good workplace habit is to always double-check your emails for grammatical mistakes, spelling errors, typos, or the all-important reply verses reply all, before hitting the Send button. Even good habits taken to an extreme can become bad habits.

Recent research has shown us that habits are part of the way we are wired; they're imprinted on our brain. Habits can be difficult to change. According to modern myth it takes about twenty-one days to change a habit. I am not sure who started this myth; however, a 2010 article in the *European Journal of Social Psychology* found that the time it takes to break a habit ranges anywhere from 18 to 254 days, with an average of sixty-six days.[7] It is easiest to change a habit by forming a new one. To change a habit, we must first be consciously aware of the behavior we want to change. Then, we can try to replace the behavior with a new routine. Everyday workplace habits are easier to deal with and change than a quirky personality trait. A simple workplace habit, like going to the coffee bar at the same time every day, can easily be changed.

Have you ever thought about those bad workplace habits you would like to change? The ones that get in the way of your professional success? Interrupting someone when they are speaking can be a negative habit, which will hinder your success on the job. Can you think about a recent interaction you had on the job in which a negative habit got in the way? Being mindful of these and recognizing what they are can be a first step toward improvement. Make your own list. Spend time thinking about that list. Ask a mentor, coach, or friend for feedback. Once you get that feedback, be open to change. Setting out an action plan with specifics on how you will make the change is part of this process. It does not need to be overwhelming. Pick two or three workplace habits to begin with. Keep it simple and manageable.

Finding success on the job is difficult enough without our own bad habits getting in the way.

Are You at Your Best?

Talent is the overriding factor in the NFL.
Has been for a long time.

—**Tony Dungy,** former coach, Indianapolis Colts

In professional sports, we know it's all about winning. To win, teams must field the most talented athletes. Similarly, organizations must have talented employees at every level to succeed in business. In order to manage talent, many organizations have some form of performance management system, which often includes a ranking system. Ranking systems are intended to identify top-tier talent, or in so many words "separate the best from the rest." Current-day thinking calls this "employee segmentation"—separating employees based on categories of performance. Do you fall into the "exceeds expectation" category? Perhaps you have been slotted into the "needs improvement" category. Since our earliest school days we've been given progress reports and grades. It's no different in the workplace; we are still being graded.

Regardless of your ranking, your focus should always be on continuous improvement. Set the bar high for yourself. Think of yourself as the CEO of your own business. As the CEO, you want to hire the best and most talented, just as they do in professional sports. Would you hire yourself? If you find yourself at the bottom end of some forced ranking, use that as motivation to improve. Individual performance changes and evolves . . . it's not static.

In my business experience, I have seen many situations in which individuals were ranked in the middle or the bottom of some ranking system; when they changed companies, all of a sudden they became rock stars at the new company. Occasionally, a change in scenery is all that was needed for them to excel. The lesson learned here is this: Continued focus on self-improvement ensures success. Regardless of your situation, manage your own performance. Take the initiative yourself to grow and develop; acquire those necessary skills and experiences to take you to the next level.

Former Harvard Business School professor David H. Maister has written extensively on the management of professional service firms. Now retired, Maister was in high demand as a consultant in the late 1990s. I had the opportunity to work with him and was fascinated by his approach to categorizing professionals into three types: cruisers, losers, or dynamos. Brutal, right? People who fall into the dynamo category are deserving of this label because they are "always on their way to somewhere," according to Maister. They are at the top ten percent of any organization—the fast trackers. On the other hand, cruisers are highly competent but show up day in and day out doing the same thing without ambition to move up the ladder. They make the widgets, but high-quality widgets. All organizations need someone to run the factory; that's what cruisers do. Losers are . . . well, losers. They are the bottom ten percent of the ranking. His categorization of professionals is harsh. However, it does make you think. When you think about being at your best, are you a dynamo, a cruiser, or a loser?

Motivation

People say motivation does not last. Well, neither does bathing—
that's why we recommend it daily.... Make motivation a habit.

—**Zig Ziglar,** author and motivational speaker

The more I learn about myself, the more I'm convinced we are wired a certain way. The best way to effect change and alter those workplace behaviors getting in the way of success—such as showing up late to the office day in and day out, continually procrastinating, or constantly forgetting to double-check your work—is to channel motivation in the right direction. Are you motivated to change? For most of us, as we entered the workforce early in our career, we were highly motivated to prove ourselves and succeed. Hard work, persistence, drive to succeed, and ambition differentiated those who excelled from those who didn't. Similarly, when you think about workplace behaviors that are getting in the way of our personal success, it comes down to motivation.

Research tells us there are two types of motivation—intrinsic and extrinsic. Individuals motivated by *extrinsic factors* expect something in return for their actions—a reward of some kind. These individuals get up every day and go to work expecting to be paid for their efforts. Their motivation is the reward of compensation. *Intrinsically motivated people*, on the other hand, are by their nature naturally motivated. They are curious and have a desire to learn, excel, and better themselves. In the real world of career management, both types of motivation are important because they play out each and every day. External factors do motivate and drive us, but having a natural orientation toward motivation is equally important.

As you strive to better yourself and achieve your goals, make sure you channel motivation. A note of caution here: Motivation in and of itself often will not get the job done. You must be motivated and realistic at the same time. For example, I'm a runner—a pathetically slow one, but I enjoy getting outside and running. I also like to compete in races. Regardless of whether it's a 5K, 10K, or longer distance, I'm never going to win my age group, no matter how motivated I am or how hard I train. I still compete, but I set goals that are obtainable. Often a change in strategy, approach, or goal is the key to channeling that motivation in the right direction. Motivation along with incremental goal setting is critical when trying to make a change. Your goals should be clearly defined, measurable, and attainable. As motivational speaker and author Zig Ziglar wisely advises, "Make motivation a habit."

Performance Reviews

Success is not final; failure is not fatal.
It is the courage to continue that counts.
—Anonymous

Performance reviews are a fact of life in business. Organizations need to evaluate performance. Sadly, reviews generally fall into two categories: bad and really bad. This is one of those workplace rituals that most of us dread. From a business perspective, a properly administered performance management program aligns people strategy to business strategy and, when used properly, becomes an important lever in motivating employees.

Managers are just not trained in conducting formal reviews, or they simply don't take the time to prepare for a meaningful conversation. You hear comments from managers and supervisors like, "I hate having to confront employees on underperformance because they get upset or defensive."[8] Complaints from both employees and employers are common throughout the halls of corporate America.

Performance reviews are a key part of our development and learning. On the positive side, the right conversation during a review can lead to an employee feeling like a valued part of the team. On the negative side, a poorly communicated review can lead to feelings of anger and resentment. From my experience, taking responsibility and having some ownership of the process will lead to better results. What do I mean by that?

Not being defensive during the review discussion is a start. Listen patiently and don't make excuses or argue. During the review, you will receive feedback about what you did or did not do or accomplish. Granted, some feedback may be based on totally inaccurate information, and you will want to correct the record accordingly. Always speak in a way that creates a win-win solution. Listen patiently. As your manager finishes, you can respond by simply saying, "What I hear you telling me is . . ." (Active listening! See page 98.) Restating what you hear is important to clarifying the message. It's also important to summarize the results of the review and schedule a separate follow-up meeting with your manager to review your notes.

The thing to remember is to use the information obtained during the review to your advantage. Regularly schedule a meeting with your boss to gauge results. In my opinion, it's best to conduct performance reviews throughout the year—daily, weekly, monthly, etc. A good manager gives feedback continuously and regularly. Ask for that.

Making Feedback Work

Feedback is the breakfast of champions.

—**Ken Blanchard and Spencer Johnson,** authors of *The One Minute Manager*

When it comes to receiving feedback, I recommend you welcome it. That's not to say it will be as helpful as it could be. While the goal of employee reviews is to improve performance, it often doesn't work out this way. These systems can become bureaucratic and routine; moreover, corporate politics often cloud what should be a clear, helpful activity.

Feedback is the most important component of the review discussion. Effective feedback must be honest and transparent, given and received in the spirit of an open dialogue.

In my coaching practice, I always encourage individuals to take the initiative to think about ways to improve their performance. Collect the feedback you receive during a review and break down the information into three categories:

1. Things you should **stop** doing: Make a list of all the behaviors that were identified as needing improvement.

2. Things you should **start** doing: Transpose the list from #1 into positive statements of what behaviors are desirable.

3. Things you should **keep** (continue) doing: All the things for which you were praised.

These three feedback categories provide an excellent way to keep things simple and help you achieve the right results.

It does not matter how many years' experience you have or how long you have been in your current role or position. There are always things we can do better. In addition, as a high achiever, you should always seek ways to improve. Focusing on those behaviors and actions you want to continue doing and those behaviors you wish to start doing is the direction you want to go. Of course, stopping bad behaviors must always be part of your improvement plan.

Focus on observable actions and behaviors. This will lead to an improved and positive work environment and to career advancement.

Dealing with Job Stress

Mind is the master weaver, both of the inner garment of character and the outer garment of circumstance.

—James Allen, *As a Man Thinketh*

I'm fortunate to live in one of the best places on the planet—Newport Beach, California. Recently while driving up Newport Coast Road toward the Pacific Coast Highway, I realized, as the Pacific Ocean came into view across the horizon, how soothing the sea can be. It has a real calming effect. As we work on ways to deal with workplace stress, the paradox of the ocean is an excellent way to think about it. On occasion the ocean can be turbulent and treacherous, but once the storm and winds subside, it will ease back into a rhythmic, soothing sea of blue.

Let's face it—work is stressful; it can be turbulent and difficult. Whether you are dealing with corporate politics, a difficult boss, disgruntled coworkers, or missed project deadlines—all of this can lead to job stress. While we can't control others and events, we can change how we think and react to them, which may lead to a more favorable outcome. James Allen's tiny book *As a Man Thinketh* contains many messages that can help us deal with job stress. His message is simple: How we think about events and situations will dictate their outcomes in our lives.

In thinking about ways to cope with job stress, I have four guidelines I try to live by:

- **Communicate, communicate, and communicate.** As workplace events happen, don't bottle them up and go into seclusion. Seek the counsel of a trusted advisor at work. Speak to a friend, partner, spouse, mentor, or coach about what's going on. Seeking the advice of these individuals can help relieve the stress, and they can likely give you valuable feedback on how to deal with each circumstance.

- **Focus on the bigger picture, not the small minutiae.** All of us should have both short-term and longer-term career plans. In dealing with ongoing workplace issues, always ask yourself, "How does this fit in with both goals?" Don't lose sight of your longer-term goals.

- **Learn to let go.** We cannot control outcomes. We can control our ability to let go and not sweat the small stuff.

- **Exercise regularly.** Find passion outside of work in some form of exercise. Get your heart rate up! Sweat! It's good for the soul and leads not only to physical health but to emotional health as well.

Unfortunately we cannot eliminate job-related stress altogether, but we can develop better skills and tools for dealing with it.

Avoiding Termination

Anticipating the loss of a job is like
choosing the best way to be hit by a truck.

—William J. Morin, *Parting Company*

"I'm letting you go."

How many times have you heard these words spoken throughout the halls of corporate America? Being fired is a painful experience and can destroy your identity. As the quote states, it's similar to being hit by a truck. It can often lead to self-doubt and depression. In fact, social science research tells us that the three most traumatic separations in our lives can stem from divorce, the death of a loved one, and losing your job.

In today's economy, losing your job for any reason is much more commonplace; many people experience being let go. It does not carry the stigma it once did. C-level executives and all ranks of professionals lose their jobs. However, losing your job does not need to be as traumatic as it once was. There are ways we can ease the pain of being terminated, and they start with you, the individual. You can't just quit life because you feel defeated in your career.

Here are some ideas to help you deal with impending or actual job loss:

- **Be prepared.** Don't get blindsided. Pay attention to the organizational signals being sent to you. Use this information as an opportunity to improve. Don't rely on others to take control of your career. Look at your employment status with the organization as a one-year employment agreement, renewable annually. Each year, ask yourself these three questions:

1. Are you continuing to learn and progress professionally?

2. Does your current role continue to keep pace with your long-term goals?

3. Do you like the team and people you're with?

Positive answers to these questions should lead you to commit to another year. Most importantly, have a backup plan in case things go awry.

- **Always upgrade your skills and experience.** As professionals we must be continuous learners, acquiring new skills and tools to help us progress in our careers. Volunteer for a new project at work, keep abreast of what's new in your field, and use this information to your advantage.

- **Network, network, and network.** This is probably self-explanatory but often undervalued by all of us. The contacts in your network are your number-one best asset. Use LinkedIn and other lists. Learning to use your contacts effectively is a very powerful tool in managing your career. Speak at industry conferences, or take a leadership role in your professional association. These activities will expand your network exponentially.

Individuals you know and socialize with in both your industry and your social network are invaluable to you as you progress through your career. In times of need, like losing a job, they can provide the lifeline to greater success.

Managing Your Manager

The most important single ingredient in the formula of success is knowing how to get along with people.

—Anonymous

The relationship with your boss is the most important relationship of all workplace relationships. Most of us would agree that a bad relationship with the boss equates to a bad work experience. Let's face it—good bosses are hard to find. If you have a poor relationship with your boss, there are steps you can take to try to improve the situation, which will be more productive than quitting and finding another position. It's in your best interest to look for ways to make things better.

I call this my four-point plan to help you "manage your manager" and create a better working relationship:

1. **Isolate two or three specific workplace behaviors that the boss engages in that bother you.** Once you have done this, try to identify steps you can proactively take to reduce their negative effects on you. For example, if your boss is continuously giving you vague instructions and expecting you to take action on less than a full set of facts, always seek clarification. If the boss doesn't give you enough face time to do that, try email. Also, looking at your own behavior and responses to issues can provide some insight on different ways to deal with negative behavior.

   Increase face time with the boss. To help create a positive working relationship, request regular meetings with the boss, either weekly or biweekly. The idea here is to ensure that you and the boss are in synch with one another. Face time is important in the corporate world, but you must manage this time wisely. Be prepared. Don't waste this time by wasting your boss's time. Becoming more efficient is the way to increase the value of face time.

2. **Accept feedback.** Embrace constructive feedback as a means to improving the relationship. Don't take negative feedback personally; it's intended to facilitate learning and improvement. On the flip side, don't blindly accept unfair and baseless criticism. You may need to push back on occasion—without being defensive. Knowing when to push back can be tricky, but it helps if you start by asking clarifying questions, or offering another approach. If your boss tells you, for example, that you need to take the initiative more often, and yet she's criticized you for moving forward on things, you probably feel confused. Rather than starting out by defending your behavior, ask her to clarify how she perceives the difference between taking the initiative and waiting to get her permission.

3. **Maintain a visible and strong work ethic.** I'm not suggesting we merely increase the number of hours we work; I'm suggesting we work smarter, with an increased focus on efficiency—getting more done in our workday.

4. **Always aim to do your best and operate at a high level.** Strive for excellence at all times. As the comedian Steve Martin once said, "Be so good they can't ignore you." Your boss will recognize this.

Not every sour relationship with the boss is salvageable. However, following these simple steps will help improve the dynamics between you and your manager.

The Know-It-All

It is impossible for anyone to begin to learn
that which he thinks he already knows.

—Epictetus, Greek philosopher

During my corporate career, I witnessed just about every version of annoying workplace behavior. The most difficult was the know-it-all. At some point in our career we all end up working with someone like this, or even worse, we may find ourselves working directly for someone like this—the person who simply knows everything. This is the arrogant, stubborn, know-it-all-type person who must show everyone how smart they are. Marshall Goldsmith, in his book *What Got You Here Won't Get You There*, describes it this way: "Being smart turns people on. Announcing how smart you are turns them off."[9] So, the real question is, how do you deal with this behavior? This is not easy, and there are no simple answers. You can simply ignore it, but that often does not help and can perpetuate the behavior. By force of will, you can't change people or mandate a change in personality. This is difficult.

If you are willing to take some risks, there are steps to consider. First, it's important to approach the topic objectively and constructively, without becoming too personal. The know-it-all personality type often seeks and needs validation. That's what drives their behavior. An approach to dealing with this might start with acknowledging that their information or position has merit, then immediately following with other ideas worth considering. Have your facts in hand. Stand your ground without being bullied or bullying.

Feedback is also a powerful motivator. Give the know-it-all direct feedback about this behavior. You should not describe it as annoying, but rather explain it as offensive and off-putting. You also may have the opportunity to participate in a 360-degree feedback process, in which colleagues and subordinates are asked for specific feedback on a person. This is normally done anonymously, and at times through a third party. Organizations will do this to develop a comprehensive assessment of the person's strengths and weaknesses; this can be your opportunity to offer feedback without fear of retaliation.

At the end of the day, there are no easy answers to dealing with these types of individuals. But helping people to discover some insight on their own is a good place to start.

Managing Egos

If you're going through hell, keep going.

—Douglas Bloch, self-help author and counselor

Dealing with egos or, worse yet, working directly for an egomaniac can be difficult and challenging—at times it can seem like slow torture. I know; I have been there. These are the types of individuals who will always begin their sentences with the proverbial "However, . . ." to show how smart they are. At some stages of our career, we are willing to tolerate different levels of stress and frustration, like working for an egomaniac, in order to reach our ultimate goal.

Yet I would not suggest we give up—that we just lie down and do nothing. Dealing with egos in the workplace is a bit like dealing with bullies in the schoolyard. You must outsmart them. The one lesson I learned from my experience is never to keep score with these folks. Individuals with oversized egos are often insecure and plagued with feelings of inadequacy and self-doubt; so keeping score only makes the situation worse. Another point worth mentioning: People who think they are the center of the universe are not the smartest people in the room; they just *think* they are.

Here are some helpful hints on dealing with egos:

- My first word of advice, right out of the gate, is to accept them for who and what they are; you will not change them!

- When devising a strategy to deal with egos, it's important to always "be prepared." It's like getting up in the morning and doing an hour of hard cardio just to get mentally prepared to deal with the drama of each day. Earlier in my career, I spent many years working for a major Wall Street firm and dealt with many different egos. We used to say informally that getting mentally prepared to handle all the investment bankers' egos we had to deal with was like preparing to "bite the head off a gorilla." Focus, focus, focus.

An excellent book on dealing with difficult people is *Bullies, Tyrants, and Impossible People* by Ronald Shapiro and Mark Jankowski. The authors explain how the level of focus required to deal with egos is similar to the focus required of an athlete. I like this. The focus of a Kobe Bryant or Serena Williams is needed. In the competitive workplace, people who prepare succeed.

I once worked for a senior leader whose wife treated me as though I was her personal attaché, on call 24/7 to handle her every need and request. Needless to say, this was a difficult situation. However, I learned some valuable lessons through this experience about dealing with and managing egos. My three-point plan based on this experience is as follows:

1. **Show respect, act professional, and be available to help.** Don't constantly push back, argue, or appear to be too busy to deal with them or their situation.

2. **Focus on excellent performance.** When you operate at a high level, with flawless performance and execution, you are showing you are competent, capable, and good at what you do.

3. **Demonstrate loyalty.** Don't talk behind the person's back or complain to others about how difficult they are. This will backfire on you. The workplace is filled with gossip and negative small talk. If you are having difficulty with someone, don't sound off at work about your frustrations. Speak in confidence with your partner, spouse, or coach.

Dealing with egos is not easy. There is no silver bullet or perfect way to solve all workplace issues. My experience proves that finding simple solutions will go a long way toward improving most situations.

Operating Style

The reasonable man adapts himself to the world;
the unreasonable one persists in trying to
adapt the world to himself.

—George Bernard Shaw, Irish playwright

Operating style is a combination of your demeanor, communication style, and attitude toward work-life balance, all of which will affect your success. It begins with self-awareness. Be self-aware enough about your style to consider how others might perceive you, thinking of ways you can adapt your style to improve how well you work with those around you. Take an inventory of what you believe your style to be. Are you driven, or do you lack motivation and need others to motivate you? Do you like to work alone, or are you a team player? Do you live for the organization, or are you on the other end of the spectrum and spend most of your time planning your next vacation? How would your coworkers answer the question "What kind of person is _____?" if they were asked about you?

Ask yourself some probing questions:

- Are you the jokester who has a hard time being serious? Or are you so serious and methodical that you never crack a smile?

- Do you get along well with others? Do your coworkers and colleagues look up to you and seek out your advice on difficult workplace issues?

- Do you tend to dominate a conversation, or are you a good listener? Are you so passive that you are afraid to have a voice in a conversation?

- Do you insist on controlling the outcome, or are you open to debate?

- Do you avoid admitting when you make a mistake?

It can be difficult to learn from our mistakes, if we never admit to having made any. Be open to change and adapt your operating style to work well with your coworkers; even organizations must change and adapt, or they can perish. In terms of operating style, specific behaviors and actions tell the story. How you operate can be a catalyst for success! How?

For example, your communication style can have an important impact on how others perceive you. Speak with passion, clarity, and purpose. Thinking before speaking will send a different signal than always blurting out the first thing that comes to mind. Are you able to adapt your style to fit the situation? First you must be aware of your own style; then you can adapt it to fit with a given situation. If you are the jokester who enjoys making everyone laugh, cutting up during a strategy meeting may frustrate others who are intent on accomplishing a plan by the end of the meeting.

Nonverbal communication is another important form of your operating style: how you sit in meetings, your use of hand gestures, whether you roll your eyes when you disagree with someone or something.

In addition to your communication style, your attitude toward work-life balance is part of your operating style and will impact your success on the job. While you should not put the job above all else, you should show that you are committed; you should show up every day to give your best. I once worked with a guy who called in sick only on Fridays. It definitely sent a message to employers that he was not serious about the job.

The corporate gossip is another problem area. Try not to be known as "someone in the know" when it comes to office gossip.

People who have been in the workforce for a long time understand that to be successful, we need to constantly evaluate our operating style and make necessary changes to improve working relationships with the people around us. Your operating style is how you show up every day and communicate, verbally and nonverbally. Is your style holding you back? If so, it's time to think about changing it.

Good Boss/Bad Boss: A Personal Journey

The person who knows *how* will always have a job.

The person who knows *why* will always be the boss.

—**Diane Ravitch,** former US assistant secretary of education

We all have experienced the joys of working for someone we respect, trust, and appreciate, a boss who challenges us and supports us at the same time. On the flip side, we have also experienced the horrors of working for "Attila the Hun." The difference is night and day. Over my working career I have worked for both and all varieties in between.

What I have learned is that difficult bosses are difficult because they are just difficult people. They are not transformed at 8:00 a.m. when they walk into the office and all of a sudden transform back to their regular self and pleasant personality when they leave the office. For these bosses, being difficult is a 24/7 personality trait. Yes, bad workplace bosses, like the rest of life's difficult people, can make every day a long slog.

During my working career, I have identified five essential competencies that constitute a good boss. Bosses who don't have these fall out of my "good boss circle." First, let me explain what I mean by "competency." Merriam-Webster defines *competence* as "the quality or state of being functionally adequate or of having sufficient knowledge, judgment, skill, or strength (as for a particular duty or in a particular respect)."[10] Translating that to the workplace, my broader definition includes specific behaviors that encompass knowledge, skills, abilities, and personal characteristics that differentiate superior performance from average performance. My five absolutes include—

1. **Intelligence:** A good boss is a smart boss. They must understand the business and have technical competence. This is someone who has the ability to cut through the noise and politics to get to the heart of the issue. I'm not just referring to IQ here. The person must have a high degree of emotional intelligence, or EQ. This is a boss who understands the views and perspectives of others—someone who is self-aware and capable of adapting their influencing style according to different situations and audiences.

2. **Presence:** A good boss must have presence. They are in control. They are a role model and inspire confidence in others. You know this when you see it and experience it.

3. **Vision:** A good boss must have vision, which includes clarity of purpose. This is a person capable of articulating the vision of where the organization is headed and how that applies to you. They also provide specific ways for you to make an impact and create value. This is someone with the ability to stand back from the action and look at the bigger picture.

4. **Communicator:** A good boss must be an effective communicator. This is someone who presents information clearly, with confidence, and is in control of his or her emotions. This is not the person who barks out directions. We have all experienced the screamer—clearly someone not in control.

5. **Character:** A good boss must have character. This is someone with integrity. This boss puts the interests of the organization and employees ahead of their own. It's okay to be ambitious and hard charging, someone who sets a high bar for excellence. However, a good boss is caring, respectful, and clear about their principles.

Using these five absolute characteristics, I want to take you on a personal journey through some of my bosses during my working career and describe how I managed through the difficult ones and learned from the stellar ones.

My first job out of college was as a staff recruiter, supporting the college recruiting function. I worked directly for the head of employment at a very large energy services company. This individual, let's call him Bob, had been with the organization for about ten years. Bob had passion for what he did. He inspired his staff. He put the company's goals and interests ahead of his own. While driven and ambitious, he cared about his staff and took time to train, develop, coach, and mentor. I learned a lot from him. What a great experience it was for me, as someone right out of college, to work for someone like this.

Then life got difficult. After several years in this position, I transferred into another HR role within the broader HR department, working for the same organization, just a different boss. I went to work for Andy—"Andy the politician," we called him. Andy was always looking over his shoulder, unsure of how to act, lead, or interact with his staff. He played favorites and did not think twice about doing it. That was just who he was. He was uncomfortable in his own skin, someone you could not trust. He was smart and had technical expertise; however, his lack of character overshadowed everything else. It was difficult to learn from Andy because of his lack of integrity.

What I did learn from this bad boss was the importance of always striving to perform at a very high level. If you are good at your job, these difficult bosses cannot overlook superior performance. Also, I never stooped to his level. Surviving in organizations requires you to be politically smart, but you don't need to be a disingenuous politician. Working for the politician boss can be challenging, but it need not be fatal. Standing firm with your ideas and position is very important. The politician boss will sway with the wind; but don't allow yourself to do the same, as the master politician will turn it against you.

Another bad boss I had was the "bully" boss. Gavin was always looking for someone else to blame. He was never at fault, because he was always right. These individuals are challenging, but there are ways to deal with them. One of the best books I have read on this topic is *The Blame Game* by Ben Dattner. He describes the pattern of "blame or be blamed," which is a disastrous individual trait. From my experience in dealing with the bully boss, you must *always* have your facts; and once you have them, you need to stand your ground and confront the person positively. At times, you have to hit back. This must be done tactfully—without emotion, but with confidence. Positive confrontations can happen and must happen with the bully boss. Remember, have your facts and stand your ground. Over time, I found the bully boss becoming less of a bully when I had my facts and stood my ground.

Another difficult boss is the micromanager. We have all worked for them. This is the individual who gives you an assignment and fifteen minutes later shows up at your desk asking whether you have completed it. Alice was my micromanager. In every way measurable, she met my criteria for the "good boss" designation. She was extremely smart; she had vision and presence. Alice, however, had a couple of flaws that made working for her difficult—her communication style and her tendency to micromanage. I learned a great deal from Alice during the time I worked for her, the most important being how to deal with a micromanager. I learned how to ask for specific deadlines, to reinforce these with her, and to communicate regularly as to my progress.

As I was given a project, assignment, or task, I would always ask what Alice's deadline was—the due date. Yes, the date may change, but I always had her tell me what she had in mind. At times, we negotiated the details; but I soon learned to have the micromanager communicate her view of the deadline. I worked backward from there. This requires you to be at the top of your game, constantly reminding the boss that you have it under control and will deliver as expected based on the previously communicated deadline and timeline. I found that once the boss understood this very efficient process, the micromanaging stopped.

Midway through my career, I had the joy and pleasure of working for a leader who absolutely hit the ball out of the park in terms of meeting my five competency requirements. He had them all. This person had the skills and finesse of the best CEOs you read about. I was lucky to be able to work with him. I benefited from this experience in numerous ways; the most important benefit was shaping my own management style and approach. When you have good mentors, they can provide you with lifelong lessons.

What did I learn? First, I learned the value of social competency, which is the ability to get things done through others by motivating them to succeed. As you grow and develop and take on the responsibility of managing others, social intelligence is critical. Second, I learned the value and joy that comes with developing others. All good managers must take seriously their roles in influencing the success of their staff. There's no way for us to single-handedly create a scenario of success with every individual, but we can communicate the criteria and performance expectations and create a positive culture in which every employee can succeed. The rest is up to them.

I once read that we should never waste a good opportunity to learn from a bad boss. Over my long working career, I have learned from all my bosses.

What Is Leadership?

A leader is best when people barely know he exists....
When his work is done, his aim fulfilled,
they will say, "We did it ourselves."

—Lao-Tzu, Chinese philosopher

At some point in your career, you have worked for a great leader. You know it when you see it. This is someone who expects the best from his or her subordinates, is quick with praise, but is even quicker to offer constructive feedback to help them improve. This is a boss who is tough but fair, someone who has high standards for themselves as well as others. Leading others with ease is a natural gift, to be sure. There is some truth to the saying that "great leaders are born." However, leadership skills can be learned, particularly skills that can make you more of a "natural" leader. Some leaders innately possess these skills, but most of us must develop them.

We all desire to work for someone capable of standing back from the action and looking at the big picture, someone with clarity of purpose and the ability to clearly communicate their standards and vision. A boss with an empathetic and supportive style, who is willing to learn from others, is at the top of our list.

In my years of corporate experience, I have developed some very practical views of successful leadership. A good leader must—

- **Have self-confidence and competence.** Leaders who display a lack of self-confidence are giving signs to their subordinates that the leadership duties are beyond their capabilities.

- **Understand the value of others.** Leaders hire competent staff to complement their own shortcomings. They identify talent and take a personal interest in that person's success. Good leaders have the ability to put the right individual in the right job and position, to give them the experience they need for their growth and development. Successful leaders must have an interest in people. They see themselves as a catalyst to getting things done through others.

- **Be willing to admit mistakes and be open to learning from others.** It takes maturity to admit when you're wrong, and good leaders know this. The value of learning from mistakes shows courage and humility. Learning from mistakes makes a good leader a **better** leader.

- **Be a good listener and have the patience to deal with conflicts and difficult personalities.** Because they value their staff, good leaders know it's worth taking the time to make the workplace harmonious.

- **Be a good communicator to articulate their vision, values, and strategies.** Leaders are the architects of culture. They command the room when speaking and communicate with confidence and authority.

What Is Success?

Success is not the key to happiness.
Happiness is the key to success.

—Albert Schweitzer, German theologian, philosopher, and physician

Most of us measure success along a vertical path, moving up the career ladder on the fast track. This line of reasoning can, and often does, lead to disappointment. Yet it seems that today's society believes that success equals upward mobility and making more money. I want to propose a different view of success.

In the book *Downshifting: Reinventing Success on a Slower Track*, author Amy Saltzman articulates a different view of success, one that is not necessarily tied to a particular employer, profession, or social status. Success can come in many forms. The serial entrepreneur, independent contractor, artist, janitor, furniture maker, stay-at-home mother—all of these endeavors can lead to success. Frequently, we allow what we do for a living to define us. There is nothing wrong with that. However, taken to the extreme, it can lead to frustration. I lived and worked in Japan for five years.

Culturally, Japanese workers really identify with their employers, in fact often introducing themselves in a manner such as "I'm Kamiya-san from Mitsubishi Motors," as if they are one and the same. Looking to our employer, or profession, or social status for one hundred percent of our satisfaction and fulfillment can lead us to a dead end. That inevitable restructuring and/or downsizing can change our situation overnight.

Generation Y is looking for more work-life balance, which is wonderful. They are sometimes referred to as generation **me**. However, what they seek is a more meaningful philosophy of life and career. What I love about the generation Y population (born during the 1980s through 2000) is their focus on work-life balance. They are willing to make sacrifices for their careers, but working 24/7, day in and day out, is not as accepted as it once was. The baby boomer generation accepted personal sacrifices as a way of life. For that generation, work formed the basis of a person's identity. Hard work paid off through retirement, when the company continued to take care of their retirees.

In contrast, I like the feel of today's generation. Personal time is very important. Today's generation is more efficient, and it's not all about their mastery of technology. It does not matter what you do for a living—whether you're a plumber, doctor, teacher, or accountant. As you start each workday and each workweek, look for opportunities and situations to be more efficient. Rather than just going through the "motions" of work, become more mindful of your own efficiency or lack of efficiency.

We can learn from our grown children and grandchildren; maybe it's time to listen to the younger generation for some answers.

Practice

Practice does not make perfect.
Only perfect practice makes perfect.

—**Vince Lombardi,** legendary football coach

Have you ever thought about what it takes to really get good at something? As a recreational triathlete, I'm in awe of the annual world championship Ironman event held on the big island of Hawaii. Dave Scott, the six-time winner of this grueling event, is obviously genetically gifted. However, he achieved what he did through endless training and practice. I had the opportunity to hear him speak once, and he showed a video clip on how he trained back in the 1980s when he was in his prime. His intense training schedule focused on both the physical preparation and the mental preparation needed to succeed for Ironman racing. Interestingly, at his peak, he followed a strict vegetarian diet. He took preparation to a new level. Ask any professional athlete or Olympian what the secret to their success is, and they will tell you practice, practice, and more practice.

In my experience, this also applies to business professionals and successful people in all fields of expertise. Ask any senior business leader about their secret to success and you will get many different answers, but rarely will you hear "practice" or "preparation." The reality is they did not get to where they are by accident. Practice is, I believe, something we must focus on as we move forward in our careers. If you want to get better at something, you must practice. One way to put this principle to work is to identify one professional activity you want to get better at—maybe it's making better presentations or becoming a better manager of projects or people. Pick something you have a passion for and need to improve on.

Make a plan to improve. Set steps in motion to get you there. You will get better and your career will benefit.

In the words of legendary UCLA basketball coach John Wooden, repeating a common saying from when he was a boy, "Failing to prepare is preparing to fail."

A Seat at the Table

We all should know that diversity makes for a rich tapestry,
and we must understand that all the threads of the
tapestry are equal in value no matter what the color.

—Maya Angelou

Recently, diversity and inclusion have become important strategic priorities for all businesses. Not a day goes by when you don't see something in the press or media on this topic. Diversity, inclusion, and equal pay are topics that require attention and focus. A recent survey by career website Glassdoor found that fifty-seven percent of people surveyed thought their company should be doing more to increase diversity in the workplace.[11] The same survey showed that forty-one percent of those surveyed felt their organization did not have a diverse executive team. Staggering statistics, I'd say, considering this survey was conducted in 2014. We have not made as much progress as you would think. That's why I was pleased to see the 2013 announcement from General Motors, the large multinational auto manufacturer, when they promoted a female to the position of CEO. Mary Barra, a thirty-year veteran with the company, is the first female CEO in GM's history! She previously ran GM's global human resources; so she understands the importance of people and talent development, important skills to have in the CEO position. Even in today's environment, women have struggled to reach positions of senior management. It's better than it was in the 1960s and 1970s, but we still have a long way to go. In writing about this promotion, *The Wall Street Journal* reported that just 4.2 percent of Fortune 500 chief executives are female[12]—that's fewer than five percent, mind you. Not a very positive statistic.

Admittedly, the corporate landscape continues to change, but women professionals and executives still face challenges their male counterparts do not. Gaining credibility and proving themselves is still tougher for females. Women face even greater challenges balancing their professional and personal schedules, as childrearing often plays into the equation. Luckily, companies are now beginning to implement more family-friendly policies that promote a better work-life balance.

Promoting on the basis of merit rather than gender should be the goal for all organizations. GM's decision to promote Mary Barra is a positive step in the right direction.

What Is Retirement?

I will keep working until about five years after I die.

—Warren Buffett

Okay, I'll admit it; I'm over fifty years of age and also a member of AARP (formerly the American Association of Retired Persons). This quote is from an interview with Warren Buffett in the AARP magazine.[13] I love this quote! Funny thing, though—while I'm a member of AARP, I don't believe in retirement. (However, membership does include good discounts with several retailers.)

Over the years, I have worked with many middle-aged professionals in transition. They had either been pushed out of their organization or just chose to leave voluntarily so they could think about life and ponder what to do next. Whether you are in your forties, fifties, or sixties, if you are thinking about retirement, don't. Instead, redirect. I think of transitions in life as opportunities to redirect in some way. Redirecting is synonymous with staying active and involved, which is vital for keeping the brain functioning. Consulting, starting a small business, working part-time, and being actively involved in a charity aligned with your passions are examples of ways to redirect.

As humans, we must stay active to keep things functioning. Transitions can be rewarding and fulfilling. However, you don't want to transition into doing nothing. You can only play so much golf, tennis, or whatever your hobby of choice is. Those who have highly driven, "type A" personalities might need more than hobbies to fill their days and provide some sense of purpose and involvement. There are too many things to do in life to just stop contributing when we reach a certain age.

The late Frederic Hudson, in his book *The Adult Years*, discusses the concept of the "self-renewing" person. There are many ways we can "recycle" ourselves during the course of a lifetime. Embrace the opportunity that comes with each transition in life. This can be a great time to turn the page to the next chapter and redirect to an entirely new challenge.

Don't retire; redirect!

REDIRECTING AT ITS BEST: PAUL

Paul is a good friend of mine who spent twenty-seven years as an executive working for a global airline, joining right out of college. Because of his time and service, he was eligible for an early retirement package the airline was offering. They were looking for volunteers, and Paul took them up on the offer. At fifty-two years old, he did not want to retire and was exploring his options and thinking about what to do with the rest of his life when his sister approached him about a business opportunity. His sister had heard about a manufacturer who needed a US-based representative to sell their product, which was manufactured abroad. During his tenure with the airline, he spent his entire career in purchasing. Paul understood marketing, sales, and distribution, which were key to having success in this entrepreneurial endeavor. He established a very successful business in the United States as an exclusive manufacturer's representative. In fact, the business was such a success, he brought his adult daughter in to help run the business. At age sixty-nine, Paul is still going strong.

Another example of redirecting is Robert, an insurance executive who also took an early retirement package at age fifty-five to pursue his passion for making custom wood furniture, something that he had done for twenty years as a hobby. Along with his son, Robert, who had a marketing background, he turned this business into an overnight success.

Redirection, not retirement.

Personal Growth Strategies

They themselves are makers of themselves by virtue of the thoughts which they choose and encourage.

—James Allen, *As a Man Thinketh*

Trust

The way to learn whether a person
is trustworthy is to trust him.
—**Ernest Hemingway**

Recently, one of my coaching clients was promoted to a higher-level position with increased responsibilities. Naturally, she expected a salary increase to come with the promotion. After waiting several weeks for her manager to say something, my client inquired about her salary adjustment. She was told her salary would be reviewed at year-end when the company's annual review process took place. Naturally, she was disappointed and immediately called me for guidance.

Salary adjustments for many organizations are done annually and must fit within their corporate calendar and pay-review cycle. I asked her how she felt about her situation; she responded she was discouraged and unsure as to the right course of action. My advice to my client, be patient, continue to operate at a high level, and wait until the salary review process takes place. Take the high road, but make the point with your boss that you expect to be taken care of at the appropriate time with a salary that is consistent with your new responsibilities.

These kinds of scenarios play out regularly in the workplace. The fact pattern may change based on each situation, but we often find ourselves in the dilemma of not knowing when to speak up.

Standing up for yourself is important. Be vocal about your views. A passive, mild-mannered reaction will get you nowhere. Always make your views known to your boss in a professional manner. In effect, you are putting the boss on notice. This scenario is the ultimate "trust me" trade, and most of the time it's the sensible approach to take. It gives the boss and organization time to make good on a promise. However, remember the new realities of corporate loyalty. You, and you alone, are responsible for managing your career and its direction, not the company. Keep in mind that if at the end of the year the organization does not do the right thing and adjust your salary in accordance with your increased responsibilities, perhaps it's not the place you want to be to build a long-term career.

There was a positive outcome to this example. My client did accept the delayed salary adjustment. She also respectfully let her boss know her expectations. In effect, he was put on notice. At year-end, she was given a significant pay increase that corresponded with her increased level of responsibility and reflected her earlier promotion—a valuable learning experience with a successful conclusion.

What Is Character?

Personality can open doors,
but only character can keep them open.

—**Elmer G. Leterman,** author and salesman

Personality plays an important role in getting a job, but character is extremely important in building and sustaining your career. Successful careers are built on a solid foundation of character. It does not matter what you do for a living; without strong character, your actions and behaviors will eventually catch up with you and produce negative results.

How does this play out in the workplace? In several ways. First, are you someone who stands by your word and commitment? Do you treat peers, colleagues, and clients with professional courtesy and respect? Do you admit mistakes rather than blame others? These behaviors play out regularly in our everyday business transactions.

Many organizations have corporate values that are inspirational in nature. They even use language pointing to honesty and integrity. A perfect example of this is Four Seasons Hotels, of which I am a big fan. That hospitality company lives the values it espouses. When you go to their website, you will find their values, beliefs, and principles listed right up front. These values are instilled into the culture and guide the actions of all their employees.

On the other hand, I recently consulted with an organization struggling with significant staff turnover, where corporate values were not clearly defined and conveyed. I interviewed a large number of employees. As a result, I found that the corporation's core values were not clearly articulated throughout the organization. In my experience, institutionalizing these values is not that easy. Leadership will drive the results. Without top-down management focused on these values, they will simply not be part of the corporate culture. I met with the CEO and asked him to describe his view of what success meant at the company and what he expected from his employees. I then asked him to tell me about his management philosophy. I recommended they develop a clearly written communication strategy regarding the company's values and that they regularly schedule meetings to convey these values to employees.

Always embrace character as part of who *you* are and how *you* operate. Don't wait for someone to force it on you. Embracing character on your own will pay significant dividends as you navigate the ups and downs of your career.

What Can Coaching Do for You?

People participate in or seek out coaching
because they want things to be different.
—**Henry and Karen Kimsey-House,** *Co-Active Coaching*

During my career I have seen situation after situation in which organizations promote someone into a new role with increased responsibilities and just assume that person has all the qualifications and skills needed to succeed in the new role, without providing any additional training. However, over the past several years the practice of professional coaching, both individual and organizational, has gained significant momentum. As a way to develop their high-potential employees, organizations are providing coaching to executives. Organizations navigating significant change such as restructuring and/or downsizing are turning to external coaches to help manage the change process. Individuals are also turning to coaching for many different reasons, some of which include assessing their individual management and communication style or to shore up specific weaknesses. The bottom-line goals for coaching are skills development, individual performance enhancement, self-assessment, and behavior change and improvement.

The Center for Creative Leadership describes coaching as the process of "bringing out the best in people."[1] This is an excellent way to think about the process. I think of coaching the same way I think about athletic training. In order to be proficient at some athletic endeavor, you need to train. You cannot improve without training. Likewise, if we want to improve ourselves to be more effective in the workplace, coaching can help. Coaches can help you identify strengths and weaknesses, personality traits (both good and bad), communication styles, and possible career paths and strategies.

The value of coaching is helping individuals realize they don't necessarily have all the answers. Knowing the limits of our own expertise is an important self-discovery. In fact, recognizing that you don't need to have all the answers is a very freeing experience. I have always learned from others and from hiring individuals who complement my weaknesses and shortcomings. I tried hard to not just hire another version of myself.

B. F. Skinner, the behavioral psychologist who developed the theory of "operant conditioning," proved that behavior could be manipulated through the use of positive and negative reinforcement. For example, a pigeon can be taught to press a specific lever by being rewarded with a food pellet or being shocked for choosing the wrong lever. We can't have an electric shock applied to us every time we act inappropriately or say the wrong thing to our work colleagues, our clients, or, even worse, our boss. According to Skinner's theory, the electric shock would soon change our bad behavior. Since getting shocked isn't an option (thankfully), this is where coaching comes in.

Hire a coach; it is less painful! A coach will help you recognize where and how these negative behaviors and traits are getting in your way, help you develop an action plan to deal with them, and put in place a strategy for improvement. The best outcomes I have seen from coaching relationships are when specific behaviors are identified to work on. Again, coaching is not corporate therapy. It should have a clearly defined beginning, middle, and end. Remember my comments about learning from our performance management feedback: start, stop, and continue. Coaching can bring out the best in you.

Choosing a Coach

Knowing others is intelligence;
knowing yourself is true wisdom.

—Lao-Tzu, Chinese philosopher

Choosing a coach can be a daunting task. In general, the coaching industry is in flux, because the bar for entry is low. As a practice, coaching dates back decades; its roots originated in the field of sports. For years, professional athletes and performance artists have turned to coaches to help them perform better and improve. Individual coaching is not just a one-time event; it's a continuing process. It's based on a foundation of trust. Today there are life coaches, career coaches, business coaches, executive coaches, and even cybercoaches—the list goes on.

One of the most important things to ask yourself as you select a coach is this: What do I want? What result am I seeking? Once you decide on the answer to that question, choose a coach to help you work on that issue. Easy, right? Well, as they say, the devil is in the details. Once you know the coaching issue you want to work on, finding someone who meets your requirements and expectations is not so easy.

What matters most in hiring a coach? The first hurdle is experience. Does the coach have specific experience in the area(s) on which you want to focus? The second barometer to look at is whether they have some type of coaching credential. The coach should be able to articulate his or her methodology and process. The International Coach Federation is an excellent information source on coach credentialing. Keep in mind that a PhD is not necessarily the number-one marker for a professional coach. It could be, but you need to probe. Many individuals with clinical psychology backgrounds use that as a mask for coaching. **Coaches do not treat psychological problems.** They help you move forward when you are stuck, act as a sounding board, and help you develop specific skills to improve. Their training is not in the area of diagnosing and treating psychological problems. Coaches are skilled at listening and using questions to help you come to your own conclusions. That is their value. Throughout the coaching process, they bring their own experience and perspective to each coaching situation. Finally, always ask for references. Coaching is a referral business; professional coaches will have no problem providing references. Professional coaches should have certain skills and training; you should probe to determine their qualifications.

One of the most important aspects of coach selection is personal chemistry. There needs to be some sort of connection, built on trust and mutual respect, between you and the coach. When I'm contacted by an organization about a potential coaching assignment, I insist on meeting the person first to determine fit. It works both ways. Both parties need to be comfortable with one another, encouraging two-way communication and accountability.

The coaching experience should allow you to gain insights into yourself that are important to your personal and professional growth.

Dealing with Failure

Failure is simply the opportunity to begin again,
this time more intelligently.

—**Henry Ford,** American industrialist, the founder of the Ford Motor Company

We have all experienced failure in one way or another during our careers. Surely you've heard the saying "What doesn't kill you only makes you stronger." When dealing with past failure, as well as current disappointments—whether it's the loss of a job, not getting that promotion you wanted, not getting into the college you hoped for, or failing to receive that salary increase you expected—always remember that these events do not dictate the future. I firmly believe that past situations do not define who we are today. Many of us will have a tendency to allow disappointment and failure to define us and therefore limit our future success and potential. During my career, I have worked with and for individuals who believed they'd never failed in their careers. To those individuals I say, "Look again." Part of being self-aware, which is an important leadership competency, is accepting failure. Even successful CEOs of large corporations fail.

Several years ago Jill Abramson, *New York Times* executive editor, was fired from the top job, after being in the role for only three years. Her boss, the owner and publisher, forced her out. Shortly after being fired, Abramson spoke to a graduation class at Wake Forest University and told the students, "Some of you . . . know the disappointment of losing or not getting something you badly want. When that happens, show what you are made of."[2]

Thought leaders in the field of self-help have written extensively on the subject of resiliency, particularly since the financial crisis.

What does it mean to be resilient? Merriam-Webster defines *resiliency* as "recovering strength, spirit, and good humor." The ability to overcome obstacles with a positive attitude is at the heart of what resiliency is all about. Moreover, it's about letting go and moving forward.

Don't let today's disappointment and/or failure get in the way of tomorrow's success. Learn from these situations. As the saying goes, "Failure is not fatal." Words to live by, don't you think?

Failures will inevitably happen. Keeping a positive attitude with the goal of learning from the experience and not letting it define you is the right focus.

THE SEASONED EMPLOYEE WITH
MULTIPLE RESUMES: MATTHEW

Matthew was a seasoned consumer product professional with twenty years in the business. Having worked at only two organizations during that time, he never had to really "look" for a job. Yet after fifteen years at a global Fortune 500 consumer products organization, he was let go as a result of a corporate reorganization. Matthew then found himself in the uncomfortable position of having to seek new employment. With an Ivy League education, including an MBA from the University of Chicago, he had impressive credentials. However, he was completely uncertain about how to start his job search.

During his career, Matthew had worked in three key areas, including strategic planning, product sales, and global operations. He had a successful track record in all of these areas and planned to explore employment opportunities in each. The conundrum he faced was how to pull all this wonderful experience into a resume that adequately represented his strengths, experience, and background. As I worked with Matthew, it became obvious that the best strategy for him was to have multiple resumes that showcased his expertise in each of these areas. So Matthew developed three different resumes and used them to strategically target specific opportunities. He developed his elevator speech to mirror these different presentations of his background to ensure he was communicating the right message.

In the end, he joined another consumer product organization in product sales. This organization offered him a management role, which included a global operations component. In Matthew's case, having multiple resumes played to his background and job-search strategy.

What Is Competition?

The ultimate victory in competition is derived from the inner satisfaction of knowing that you have done your best and that you have gotten the most out of what you had to give.

—Anonymous

In business, as in sports, we compete. Externally, businesses compete for market share, revenue, and profits. Internally, employees compete for individual success, recognition, financial gain, the next promotion, and so on. This internal competition can, and often does, get in our way as we try to succeed and have positive interactions with workplace colleagues. The problems arise when competition itself becomes the focus. In my view, internal competition should not be about gaining an advantage over your opponent, as it is in sports. Rather, it's all about striving to reach your individual potential, being the best you can be, and feeling good about the end result.

Regardless of your chosen profession or trade, at the end of the day, personal fulfillment is what's important. Feeling good about your performance is what matters. Define success for yourself. Don't let anyone else define it for you. Often in business you see individuals playing what I call the "gotcha" game. Are you familiar with that game? It's the "I win/you lose" game and the mentality that goes with it. This behavior leads to negative politics and self-protection, rather than openness, transparency, growth, and learning. Sadly, many organizations thrive on this type of culture and behavior, as do some individuals.

I prefer to think of win-win scenarios in business. While we cannot control other people's behaviors, we can conduct ourselves differently and still have career success. It happens all the time. I'm not suggesting that we wimp out each and every time we encounter difficulty and adversity. We need to stand our ground, communicate with purpose, and make our voices heard. This can be done without playing the gotcha game. Political expediency, doing things just to get ahead at the expense of others, is another behavior trait not based on a win-win philosophy.

Have you "gotten the most out of what you had to give"?

Developing a Learner's Mindset

We don't see things the way they are;

we see things the way we are.

—Anaïs Nin, essayist and author

This quote has always resonated with me. Even today, the wisdom in this simple statement can have significant meaning. I often hear from friends and former colleagues who are unhappy in their jobs. They have a difficult boss, no longer support the direction of the organization, are unhappy in their current role—the list is endless. In the workplace, our mental models can either be positive or negative, depending on the situation. And sometimes it's hard to break out of those modes. Being fired, for example, can bring severe negative consequences, which can lead to negative attitudes, can lead to pessimism, and can in extreme situations even lead to depression.

I'm the first to say that often a change is exactly what's needed for someone to get a fresh start. However, in times when a job or boss change is not an option, there are ways to improve your situation. The key is to be open to instruction, to have a learner's mindset. There has been a great deal written on the topic of what it means to have a "learner" mindset. So, what does it mean to have a learner's mindset?

Marilee Goldberg introduced this concept in 1998 and refers to it as being open to changing your approach, thinking, feeling, and/ or behavior.[3] A learner mindset is oriented toward the positive and creates a mood of win-win, not one of "I win/you lose."

Carol Dweck, a Stanford University professor of psychology, recently published a book entitled *Mindset: The New Psychology of Success.* She promotes the concept that our attitude about where our talents originate—innate ability or learned ability—will affect our response to failure. Those with a "growth mindset" believe their abilities and talents are not fixed and therefore are more able to change, develop, and grow.[4] This is uplifting. The message is this: We can change direction, avoid getting stuck in neutral, and be able to veer around obstacles and roadblocks—situational, organizational, and people oriented—in the workplace, if we remain open to change.

It's important to be mindful of what you are thinking and feeling at any particular time. The most important action to take when dealing with difficult work situations is to focus on the outcome you desire and then on how you can positively influence that outcome.

When approached with a negative situation, ask yourself what you can personally contribute to moving the situation forward and toward improvement. This type of mindset and approach is more accepting of self and others. Remember, any change we wish to see has to begin with ourselves.

Job Burnout

Burnout is nature's way of telling you you've been going
through the motions but your soul has departed;
you're a zombie, a member of the walking dead, a sleepwalker.

—Sam Keen, American philosopher

I always refer to the recent financial crisis as a defining moment in the global workplace, because it was. All of us working professionals at the time felt its effects. Traumatic. I remember waking up every morning and watching the markets lose half their value. We all lost a great deal of sleep over daily events. Since the financial crisis, we have all been asked to do more with less. Longer hours have become the norm. In addition, reduced staffing levels are the new corporate reality. These factors place more pressure on us to perform, and often this increased workload comes without additional compensation. Many of us are reluctant to complain about these issues, because we are fearful of losing a job or being labeled a "complainer." All of this can lead to job burnout!

What exactly causes someone to suffer job burnout? In simple terms, prolonged stress is the answer. Do you feel overworked, undervalued, and generally underappreciated? Feelings of helplessness to change your situation can also lead you to job burnout. When employers see a gradual decline in job performance from someone who has been a top performer, this is generally a sign there may be an issue. For example, frequent sick days for someone who has never taken time off is not a good sign.

We all have good days and bad days at work. This is normal. However, physical signs like lack of sleep, feeling tired and drained, and, even worse, endless illnesses are not normal; these are signs of a bigger problem.

You don't want to "sleepwalk" through life and work; slogging through the same routine, day in and day out, in a job that may be unfulfilling and unrewarding can paralyze us and lead to inaction. So if any of this resonates with you, it's time to take control to make changes. At some point in our working career, we all feel the effects of being burned out. Unless you are dealing with severe depression or anxiety, which may require professional help, the first step in dealing with job burnout is recognizing what's going on and accepting there is a problem.

Remember that job burnout is not terminal. Taking action steps to change will lead to recovery—steps that might include taking time off from work to give yourself a chance to rest, reflect, and heal. Simply slowing down is important. Also, you cannot get better alone. Friends and family are critical to recovery. Sharing your feelings with another person will release some of the burden.

Starting each day with some form of relaxing ritual can help. Wake up early enough to write in a journal, read something inspiring, or just do some easy exercise. All of this will help you start the day with a fresh outlook. Changing your daily routine can also help. Don't overextend yourself; take regular breaks each day from your work routine to disconnect and recharge. This is important. Taking that extended vacation can be a quick way to recharge your batteries. What I mean by a vacation is just that—physically going somewhere, not just staying home to sleep! Go to the mountains, or the beach, or just take a drive across the country. It's all about getting away from the normal routine.

Lastly, re-evaluate your goals and priorities. Perhaps a job change, a career change, or even some sort of life change is in order. Find out what really makes you happy, and then develop a plan to get there.

The book *LifeLaunch: A Passionate Guide to the Rest of Your Life* by Pamela McLean and Frederic Hudson has excellent suggestions for ways to deal with life's transitions and burnout. They describe life as a series of chapters, like chapters in a book. Part of our role and destiny in life is successfully turning the page of each chapter and getting mentally and emotionally ready for the next chapter. If we find ourselves in the doldrums, as we all do once in a while, we can choose either to stay there or to turn the page in the current chapter to something new.

Regardless of the course you choose, make sure you take steps to fully recover before making any life-changing decisions.

Excellence versus Perfection

We are what we repeatedly do.
Excellence, then, is not an act but a habit.

—**Will Durant,** *The Story of Philosophy*

Have you ever thought about the difference between excellence and perfection? When I think about it, I always recall the saying "Don't let the perfect be the enemy of the good." I admit it; I'm a perfectionist. This has haunted me tremendously during my corporate career. I always strived for perfection. When it comes to career management and development, we often hold ourselves back by focusing too much on perfection. In my experience, it's the ambitious and competitive people who strive for perfection. This in itself is not a bad thing. However, it is better, and generally healthier, to instead strive for excellence.

During my career, I was global head of human resources at a large investment management organization. The firm had five core values. One of them was "Leadership and professional discipline drive us." The subtext of this value was to maintain the highest standards of excellence in all business transactions, from people to investments. I loved and welcomed the focus on excellence. Why? There is a significant difference between perfection and excellence. Striving for perfection leads to frustration. We cannot be and are not perfect. As humans, we don't work that way; by our very nature we are imperfect. Perfection is an illusion, an unattainable goal; and as long as we chase it, we will end up unhappy and confused.

However, we can strive to be excellent. Excellence is a healthy goal in which you seek to improve.

Excellence is willing to be wrong; perfection always needs to be right. Excellence is accepting and natural. Seeking perfection creates and leads to self-doubt. Keep in mind that managing your career is a marathon, not a sprint. The goal is to strive for excellence in everything you do. Excellence is being willing to take some career risks, which can lead to confidence, not arrogance.

When you have failures on the job, and you will, having the goal of excellence will help you accept failure with the right attitude. In the workplace, we all make mistakes and have disappointments. Realizing that you are not perfect enables you to be open to making mistakes and to letting those mistakes become learning experiences that lead to change and ultimately to improvement.

In the end, excellence is accepting. As Will Durant said, "Excellence . . . is not an act but a habit." Tomorrow is another day and another opportunity to do and be the best you can.

The Four Rules

Ability is what you're capable of doing.
Motivation determines what you do.
Attitude determines how well you do it.

—**Lou Holtz,** American football player and coach

Most of us have to work for a living. Hopefully, it gives you a sense of meaning, purpose, and joy. Our goal is to enjoy what we do; then it will not seem like work, right? Having spent years in the corporate world doing something I enjoyed, I still had challenges and difficult times. Let's face it: Organizations can be political and difficult to navigate. Recently, I was rereading William Bridges's book *Managing Transitions: Making the Most of Change.* He recommends following four simple rules, "show up, be present, tell the truth, and let go of outcomes,"[5] to deal with transitions. As I was thinking about these rules, I realized how useful they could be in dealing with workplace issues. Using these rules, I offer my interpretation on how they can be used to navigate difficult issues and workplace situations, which often get in the way of our own progress:

Rule 1: Show up. Whenever faced with a problem, we first need to show up. What does that mean? We need to be prepared to embrace the issue, really lean into it. Showing up means taking the time to understand the issues—including details and facts.

Rule 2: Be present. How many times have you been in a conversation with someone who seems not to be fully there? They may be there physically, but not mentally and emotionally. Whatever we face, we must be mentally present and focused. In many situations, being present is equivalent to being prepared.

Rule 3: Tell the truth. Sounds easy, and generally this goes without saying, but often the opposite is true. We have all been on the receiving end of some colleague throwing us under the proverbial bus to make himself look good. Political expediency does not lead to long-term success and eventually catches up with you. Yes, even in business, as in life, honesty is the best policy. Those who use dishonesty as they operate will eventually find themselves trapped by their own deceit.

Rule 4: Let go of outcomes. Work hard to bring change and positive results, but understand that in the end, we cannot control organizational outcomes. When we are the key decision maker, we have significant influence; but decisions often involve a number of individuals. Where we have influence, we must try to exercise it. If decisions don't go in our favor, we need to let go and move on. Holding on to resentments, grudges, or hard feelings will eat you up, from the inside out. Let go of outcomes!

The four rules—good lessons for us all.

What Is Time?

Time is the only currency we have.

—**Graham Nash**, *Wild Tales: A Rock & Roll Life*

As a fan of music, I read a lot of musicians' autobiographies. Graham Nash's recent memoir is an example. In the past several years, it seems all the aging rockers have penned one. The one common denominator in all is their realization that time is precious; the one thing we can't buy is more time! I would bet that given the choice, even the wealthiest among us would buy more time if they could. But it's not for sale; you can't buy time. Interestingly, time is an important variable in all our work activities. For example, many organizations offer training in time management for aspiring managers. These training programs are intended to train managers to use the time they have more efficiently, allowing them to get more out of their workday.

Tim Gallwey proposes an interesting perspective on the concepts of "time" and "work." He is the author of *The Inner Game of Work* and makes the point that "no one can ever succeed in managing time. If anything, time manages you."[6] Think about that for a minute. Again, *time manages us*. Gallwey says time management is a complete misnomer. This really resonated with me; time marches on—we cannot change that reality. The key is to make better use of the time we have. Gallwey defines this as becoming more "time aware."

How do we put this into practice to improve our hectic lives and workday? One way is to make a list of the tasks you need to accomplish on any given day and set a clear agenda for what needs to happen without backtracking. In my coaching work, I see essentially two groups of individuals: those who make daily lists and those who go about their day somewhat absentmindedly. I'm a list guy. I like to be organized, so I make a list. For people who make lists, how many of you look at the list at the end of each day to determine how much time it actually took to accomplish each task? Keeping in mind there are only so many hours in your workday, note the gaps in the time it actually took you to complete each task and the amount of time you thought it would take. This is how you become better at managing time. Mind-numbing, perhaps, but this exercise will provide some interesting insight into how you spend your time.

How does this all translate to managing our time at work? In my view, it's not about putting more hours in at the office; rather, it's about learning to be more efficient, as Gallwey proposes, with the time we have. As we chart our daily activities, we should focus on finding ways to be more efficient with the time we have. Even if we had an extra hour at the end of each day, what would you do with that hour? As Tim Gallwey points out, the better way to manage time is not necessarily to have more time, but to be more "time aware." During my corporate career I would see individuals walking around in a constant state of panic, always too busy to think about their busyness. Some environments promote this kind of culture. However, we don't need to accept this and can operate differently.

The fact that time marches on is another reason it's important to take control of a bad workplace situation or job. Take action instead of suffering in silence! We do not need to be unhappy; it's within our control to make the changes we need in order to solve our problems.

IQ versus EQ

In a very real sense we have two minds,
one that thinks and one that feels.

—Daniel Goleman, *Emotional Intelligence: Why It Can Matter More Than IQ*

We all know organizations want to hire smart people, but being smart is not only about IQ. Measuring how smart someone is can be done easily with the right IQ test. The Wonderlic Cognitive Ability Test is an example of a test used to measure the aptitude of prospective employees for learning and problem solving; it measures a person's cognitive ability. But, success in business and personal growth success is more than just being smart. I can't tell you how many times I have heard a senior leader say this about a candidate they interviewed: "I don't care about her experience; I just want to know, is she smart?"

What exactly does it mean to be smart?

Daniel Goleman's groundbreaking book *Emotional Intelligence* suggests there is a different way of being smart. His research showed everyone that the rules for work were changing and a different yardstick was now being used to judge individual intelligence.

Just what is emotional intelligence, or EQ? How do you know you have it, and more importantly, how do you get it if you don't already have it? At its core, EQ is about self-awareness—having the ability to control your emotions and communicate with confidence. Individuals with a high degree of self-awareness generally have a deep understanding of their emotions, strengths, and weaknesses. In addition, having the capability to read people and situations is an important part of EQ.

From my thirty years of corporate experience, this plays out daily in our work situations. EQ plays a significant role in getting hired, staying hired, and, ultimately, excelling on the job. First, to get hired you must have the requisite skills and experience. IQ does play a role here. Organizations do want to ensure you have the cognitive ability to function, compete, and excel. However, to stay employed requires social competence, or social intelligence. Knowing how to work with others and, more importantly, knowing how to get things done through others requires social intelligence. This is, to my mind, the key to defining emotional intelligence. Regardless of whatever field you choose to work in, to progress to more senior roles of responsibility you must have social intelligence. Further, the ability to deal with ambiguity and uncertainty is at the core of EQ. Individuals with a high degree of emotional intelligence are in control of their emotions. They understand how their own interpersonal behavior can impact others and those around them, and they can adjust that behavior naturally.

The good news is all of these capabilities can be learned. To some degree it's part of our wiring, but we can develop better EQ skills if we are motivated and try. At the end of the day, having success on the job and within any organization requires the ability to influence to get results. Adapting your influencing style to the situation and audience—*that's* having emotional intelligence.

Goal Setting

You are never too old to set another goal
or to dream a new dream.

—**C. S. Lewis,** British novelist, poet, and academic

We all have strengths and weaknesses. As professionals, part of our growth is continuously finding ways to improve upon our weaknesses. What is the best way to accomplish this? Whenever we try to improve on a specific behavior, we must review where we are vis-à-vis that specific behavior. This is what setting a goal is all about. The late Zig Ziglar, an author and motivational speaker, was one of the early proponents of rigorous goal setting. Many years ago I attended a seminar he gave on goal setting. I can still remember him speaking in his Texas twang about the importance of being emotionally committed to goal achievement. I always liked this idea. If we are setting our goals right, both short-term and long-term goals, there should always be a stretch goal or two on the list. A stretch goal is a goal requiring us to get outside our comfort zone. In order to achieve a stretch goal, you must be emotionally committed.

For example, suppose you want to improve your public speaking and presentation skills. That is your stated stretch goal. The first step is identifying those behaviors you engage in that get in the way of this stated goal. In the *Harvard Business Review* article "The Real Reason People Won't Change," authors Robert Kegan and Lisa Laskow-Lahey outline their research on the concept of "competing commitments."[7] These are an individual's actions, beliefs, and behaviors that continuously get in the way of that person's stated goal. During my training at the Columbia (University) Coaching Certification Program, I attended a workshop on how this research would benefit coaches in unlocking obstacles to goal setting. The ideas behind this research are intriguing. Kegan and Laskow-Lahey's research illustrates that often these competing commitments are unconscious thoughts that can prevent us from achieving our stated goals.

Using the example of improving your presentation skills, a competing commitment may be an unconscious fear of public speaking, which is getting in the way of your stated goal. In this example, this unconscious fear can and often does become your reality. It doesn't matter what your stated goal is; it's helpful to look at what competing commitment may be getting in your way.

As you go through the process of setting goals and expanding your public speaking skills, break down these goals to include what competing commitment is blocking you. The authors suggest a four-column exercise—though as you'll see in the following example, I have adapted it to three. The first column should include what the stated goal is; the second column should include any thought, action, or belief that can potentially get in the way of you achieving success— in effect any competing commitment. The third column includes the steps you will take to overcome these competing commitments. Valuable insight can be gleaned from this process. Whatever you set out to do—for example, improving your interpersonal communication skills, becoming a better project manager, and the like— make sure you understand what your competing commitments are.

Identifying Your Goal-Reaching Obstacles		
Stated goal: What you want to achieve	**Obstacles: Thoughts, actions, beliefs**	**Steps to overcome obstacles**
I want to give better presentations at work.	I am afraid of speaking in public; I fear judgment of others. I am fearful of having an anxiety attack in the middle of the presentation.	1. Prepare my material. 2. Practice alone in front of a mirror. 3. Practice in front of smaller groups. 4. Join a local Toastmasters group for more practice.

Adapted from Robert Kegan and Lisa Lahey, "The Real Reason People Won't Change," *Harvard Business Review*, November 2001, 2–9, https://hbr.org/2001/11/the-real-reason-people-wont-change.

Individual Makeup

Each person is made up of a unique combination of strengths, weaknesses, abilities, and talents, and any one of us can only truly maximize our potential in the context of that individual makeup.

—**Pete Carroll,** *Win Forever*

I love this quote from Pete Carroll because it embodies everything I believe. Pete is one of the few football coaches who has led teams to winning both a collegiate national championship and a Super Bowl. He knows a few things about winning and maximizing individual potential. What is your individual makeup? Do you know yourself well enough to articulate it?

In my career-coaching work, I spend a great deal of time on this topic, trying to help clients truly understand their own skills, strengths, and abilities. It does not matter whether you are at a career crossroads or trying to navigate your next move within your current organization; having a clear understanding of "who you are" is a key ingredient to success. This was part of the "Know thyself" phase of my career-launch strategy from section 1 of this book.

In his book *Win Forever*, Pete Carroll discusses the meaning of talent, which he defines as the sum total of a person's strengths, weaknesses, and abilities. I would take his definition a step further and add desire and passion to the equation.

Understanding yourself from this perspective gives you a significant advantage as you compete in the workplace. Why is that? Well, for one thing, once you understand what you are really competent at, you can focus on those things. Don't waste your time pursuing something if it does not play to your strengths and abilities. Individuals who truly understand their "core self" understand who they are and what makes them the person they are. For example, I'm the type of person who prefers to focus on the big picture, not the details. I can deal with details, but it's not my core strength. I know that about myself, and during my corporate career I always hired detailed people to work for me.

I look at the right career strategy as always preparing for your next job, position, and/or career move. We should be continually thinking and planning. Knowing what your individual makeup is will help you in that process.

Knowing What You Don't Know

Knowing the edge of your circle of competence is one of the most difficult things for a human being to do. Knowing what you don't know is much more useful in life and business than being brilliant.

—**Charles T. Munger,** American businessman, investor, and philanthropist

I don't know everything! Some people have a hard time admitting that. We have all worked with, and for, the person who simply knew everything. It does not matter the topic or subject—they were the experts. The pressures to succeed that we often feel in our job and career put a heavy burden on us. But the real truth is it's better to admit you don't know something than to always say you do.

All successful business leaders have their own version of how they achieved their success—their own "success story." Charles Munger, who helped Warren Buffett build Berkshire Hathaway into one of the most successful organizations in modern history, has been quoted as saying that the key to success is "knowing the edge of your circle of competence."[8] This concept really resonates with me. Success begins with knowing your limits. Brilliant!

This can be a very difficult lesson for many people. I was recently in a client meeting for a large consulting project. The topic was centered on a subject that I have some competence in, which was why I'd been invited to meet with this organization. During the hour-long meeting, the client spoke nonstop. He was like a windup toy on steroids. He spent the entire time telling me how smart he was and how he had all the answers to his problems. I got very few words into the conversation. As I left the meeting, I could not help but wonder why he'd invited me to meet with him. Clearly he didn't realize that he didn't need to have all the answers to be important.

We all have specific core competencies that make us who we are. Competencies are behaviors that define our character and style. The key to success is recognizing what these competencies are, maximizing them, and acknowledging what competencies we don't have.

In my experience, seeking advice from others, including subordinates, will yield better results than pretending that you have all the answers. It does take a certain amount of courage and humility to admit when we don't know something. I believe success begins there.

CONCLUSION

Channel Your Destiny

Life isn't about finding yourself.
Life's about creating yourself.
—Anonymous

Throughout this book I have discussed my view of continuous learning and improvement. We all must learn to adapt to the changing economic realities of the marketplace. As automobiles regularly need maintenance, we too need "maintenance" in order to stay ahead of economic and technological changes. In my view, those who do not change will end up as roadkill.

My ninety-two-year-old father-in-law remains an inspiration to me as he continues to develop and learn. He competes regularly in bridge and golf tournaments as a way to keep his brain functioning. He loves his Apple iMac computer and is constantly working to improve his computer skills. He is the epitome of a continuous learner.

Preparing this manuscript has been very cathartic for me. I wanted to share my thoughts, insights, and perspectives with a broad audience, and I hope my insights are helpful to you. My personal joy is having the ability to do what I enjoy and the opportunity to share it with others. Today's workplace has changed and will continue to change—constantly and in unexpected ways. A friend of mine works for one of the world's largest video game developers. He recently told me this organization does not have scheduled work hours; however, core hours were thought to be from 10:00 a.m. until 4:00 p.m. How times have changed! The workplace of the twenty-first century certainly looks much different from that of prior years.

Since the financial crises, organizations are forcing employees to do more with less, while allowing more flexibility. The profound changes in the business climate over the past thirty years require us to think differently about ourselves, our careers, and how we manage through the ups and downs of the economic cycles. What we have learned through the turmoil of the recent recession and downturn is that we need to rethink how we define the concept of career. We live in a world of change. The workplace is different. The contract workforce, or "contingent workforce," has become the new normal. Other nontraditional forms of employment—consulting, remote workers, project assignments, permanent part-time work, and the like—are much more the norm today. The new self-managed career does not tie us to one employer for life. With that change in definition has come the death of the psychological contract between employer and employee. Career paths today will be nonlinear, more unconventional.

All of this will lead to the growth of multiple mini-careers during an individual's working life. Remember, you are in command of your future; knock down those barriers getting in your way.

What has not changed is the fact that organizations are made up of people, and we have to work with them. We still need to interact with other humans and different personalities, and that is where the difficulty begins. Many of the challenges I faced during my career are still part of the workplace and corporate landscape today. As I tell my two adult sons, work is a privilege. To those toiling away to find joy and happiness in their work, don't give up. Resilience and determination will get you to the place you want to be. To those of you lucky enough to be in a position and career you enjoy and find rewarding, congratulations!

Embrace the future in a positive way, rather than a negative one.

In the words of Alvin Toffler, the American futurist, "Change is not merely necessary to life; it *is* life."

Additional Tips for Your New Directions Toolbox

The following includes those tips I believe are vital tools for your job-hunting toolbox. As you launch a new job search or career change, you should be mindful of these tips as a way to separate yourself from the other candidates. Amazingly, it's the simple things that often propel us to success.

Resume Preparation

Tip 1—When you write your resume, avoid the pronoun "I." Instead, use action words to describe what you did, like "coordinated," "organized," "directed," etc. Write your bullets in such a manner that clearly states what work you did. For example, "Directed a project team of fifteen who implemented a new global budgeting system."

Tip 2—Brevity is an asset. Wordy resumes will in most instances not be read and will be the first to be discarded. Keep your resume brief, concise, and to the point. It should state as clearly as possible and as concisely as possible what you did and accomplished.

Tip 3—Don't boast about unique accomplishments that are so far over the top; it seems disingenuous. For example, "I increased revenues by three hundred percent" may sound good, but first, is it true? Second, it potentially can sound pretentious and arrogant.

Tip 4—Don't use over-the-top language to explain your contribution. Using flowery sentence structure to say something simple can be seen as negative and throw you right out of contention.

Interviewing Tips

Tip 1—Arrive on time. There are simply no excuses for being late. In fact, allow extra time to get there early to get prepared and ready.

Tip 2—In most interview situations, it's advisable to dress in business attire. However, there are exceptions to this rule. Think about the right attire for the organization, culture, and position. For example, in most instances you do not need to suit up for an interview as a restaurant manager. Your dress should fit the position.

Tip 3—During the interview, don't blame others for your shortcomings. Take responsibility for your own actions. If you failed at something, admit it. There may be good reasons for not finishing a project on time and within budget. Employers appreciate honesty.

Tip 4—Show that you are motivated from the start. Organizations appreciate motivated employees. Don't appear to be disinterested.

Take charge of the process. One caution, however: Don't oversell and appear desperate. Organizations will pick up on that, and it puts you in a bad light.

Tip 5—Always send follow-up thank-you emails to each person you interviewed with, after each round. If you interviewed with numerous individuals, don't send the same thank-you email. Make sure you change them slightly. You appear to be lazy by sending the same email to every person.

Dealing with Human Resources

Tip 1—Depending on the size of the organization, the interview process will start in the human resources department. HR's role is to size up cultural fit, so many of the questions will center on this aspect. This interview will be less technical and focus on the administrative core of the company, organizational structure, key players, roles and responsibilities, and so on.

Tip 2—To make the right impression with HR, research the company and its culture. It shows your motivation.

Tip 3—In dealing with HR, approach the discussion from the position of "eagerness." Don't minimize their role in the process. "I'm eager to meet the hiring manager to discuss this position," may come off across as undervaluing HR's role in the process.

Salary Negotiation

Tip 1—When asked what salary you are seeking, never specify an amount. **Don't negotiate against yourself!** Always say you are negotiable. A statement like "I'm willing to consider any reasonable offer you make" is a good way to communicate your thinking.

Tip 2—Don't accept an offer on the spot. Always say you want to consider the offer, and then get back to them the next day. Take time to think through things. Evaluate the offer in the context of the complete package, the employee benefits, the work location, the job responsibilities, how you relate to the person you will report to, and so forth.

Dealing with External Recruiters

Tip 1—If possible, always insist on meeting the recruiter face to face. Often recruiters are not local, so a face-to-face meeting is not practical; in these instances, insist on a video interview with them. Meeting the recruiter is important to building a relationship with them and to ensuring they represent you to the potential employer in the right way. This is not just about a transaction. If the recruiter won't meet you, don't place a great deal of faith in this "relationship."

Tip 2—The way you follow up with the recruiter is important. You don't want to appear desperate, so calling every few days will have a negative effect. A regular "check-in," however, is important to keeping the dialogue going. Update them on important developments in your job search. Perhaps you received another offer you are considering, or you wanted to pass on some news about the organization you interviewed with.

Action Words to Use for Resume Development

Accomplished	Founded	Produced	Superseded
Achieved	Generated	Promoted	Terminated
Approved	Headed	Proposed	Traced
Built	Implemented	Provided	Tracked
Completed	Improved	Purchased	Traded
Conceived	Improvised	Recommended	Trained
Conducted	Increased	Redesigned	Transferred
Consolidated	Installed	Reduced	Transformed
Controlled	Innovated	Reorganized	Translated
Converted	Introduced	Rescheduled	Trimmed
Created	Instituted	Revised	Tripled
Delivered	Invented	Scheduled	Uncovered
Demonstrated	Launched	Simplified	Unified
Designed	Led	Solved	Unraveled
Developed	Maintained	Sparked	Utilized
Devised	Managed	Staffed	Vacated
Directed	Negotiated	Started	Verified
Doubled	Operated	Streamlined	Withdrew
Earned	Organized	Strengthened	Worked
Edited	Originated	Stressed	Wrote
Eliminated	Performed	Stretched	
Established	Planned	Structured	
Expanded	Processed	Succeeded	

Resources

Over the years, I've read many books that spoke to me in one way or another. The list here includes some of my all-time favorites. Keep in mind that your list will continue to grow, evolve, and change . . . just as we do.

Allen, James. *As a Man Thinketh.*

Bennett, Amanda. *The Death of the Organization Man.*

Bolles, Richard N. *What Color Is Your Parachute?*

Bridges, William. *Managing Transitions: Making the Most of Change.*

Carroll, Pete. *Win Forever: Live, Work, and Play Like a Champion.*

Christensen, Clayton M., James Allworth, and Karen Dillon. *How Will You Measure Your Life?*

Collins, Jim. *Good to Great: Why Some Companies Make the Leap . . . and Others Don't.*

Covey, Stephen R. *The 7 Habits of Highly Effective People.*

Crane, Thomas G. *The Heart of Coaching: Using Transformational Coaching to Create a High-Performance Coaching Culture.*

Csikszentmihalyi, Mihaly. *Finding Flow: The Psychology of Engagement with Everyday Life.*

Dattner, Ben. *The Blame Game: How the Hidden Rules of Credit and Blame Determine Our Success or Failure.*

Dweck, Carol. *Mindset: The New Psychology of Success.*

Dyer, Wayne. *Change Your Thoughts—Change Your Life: Living the Wisdom of the Tao.*

Frankl, Viktor E. *Man's Search for Meaning.*

Gallwey, W. Timothy. *The Inner Game of Work: Focus, Learning, Pleasure, and Mobility in the Workplace.*

Goldsmith, Marshall. *What Got You Here Won't Get You There: How Successful People Become Even More Successful.*

Goleman, Daniel. *Emotional Intelligence: Why It Can Matter More Than IQ.*

Hall, Douglas T. *Careers in Organizations.*

Hesselbein, Frances, and Eric K. Shinseki. *Be, Know, Do: Leadership the Army Way (adapted from the Official Army Leadership Manual).*

Hill, Napoleon. *Think and Grow Rich.*

Hudson, Frederic M. *The Adult Years: Mastering the Art of Self-Renewal.*

Jeffers, Susan. *Feel the Fear . . . and Do It Anyway.*

Johnson, Spencer. *Who Moved My Cheese? An Amazing Way to Deal with Change in Your Work and in Your Life.*

Kegan, Robert, and Lisa Laskow-Lahey. *Immunity to Change: How to Overcome It and Unlock the Potential in Yourself and Your Organization.*

Kimsey-House, Henry, Karen Kimsey-House, Phillip Sandahl, and Laura Whitworth. *Co-Active Coaching: Changing Business, Transforming Lives.*

Kogel, Timothy J. *The Exceptional Presenter: A Proven Formula to Open Up and Own the Room.*

Kriegel, Robert, and Louis Patler. *If It Ain't Broke . . . Break It! And Other Unconventional Wisdom for a Changing Business World.*

Lewis, Michael. *Coach: Lessons on the Game of Life.*

Lucht, John. *Rites of Passage at $100,000+: The Insider's Lifetime Guide to Executive Job-Changing and Faster Career Progress.*

McLean, Pamela D., and Frederic M. Hudson. *LifeLaunch: A Passionate Guide to the Rest of Your Life.*

Pachter, Barbara. *The Power of Positive Confrontation: The Skills You Need to Handle Conflicts at Work, at Home, and in Life.*

Saltzman, Amy. *Downshifting: Reinventing Success on a Slower Track.*

Shapiro, Ronald M., and Mark A. Jankowski. *Bullies, Tyrants, and Impossible People: How to Beat Them without Joining Them.*

Silsbee, Doug. *Presence-Based Coaching: Cultivating Self-Generative Leaders through Mind, Body, and Heart.*

Souerwine, Andrew H. *Career Strategies: Planning for Personal Achievement.*

Stanfield, R. Brian. *The Art of Focused Conversation: 100 Ways to Access Group Wisdom in the Workplace.*

Toogood, Granville N. *The Articulate Executive: Learn to Look, Act, and Sound Like a Leader.*

Acknowledgments

This book is the result of a real team effort and long journey. First, I am deeply indebted to my wife, Carol; without her advice, feedback, counsel, and support, this manuscript would never have seen the light of day. I also want to thank the individuals I have had the pleasure of working with and for during my personal journey of working. I want to also thank all my teachers, professors, friends, and mentors I have had over the years, from whom I have learned much.

I began working at the young age of fifteen, selling newspaper subscriptions. I have not stopped working since then and don't plan to stop. During high school and college, I worked in restaurants, grocery stores, in telephone sales, on construction crews, and in landscape maintenance . . . I learned valuable lessons in all these jobs. I have always felt "working is a privilege."

To my family: I have a deep gratitude to both my sons for being open to my career advice. Today, they are fully ensconced in their own careers. I'm very proud of what they have become as professionals and as individuals. I'm learning more from them than they will ever know. I'm also thankful that our family has grown to include two wonderful daughters-in-law and an awe-inspiring grandson. I am looking forward to meeting my future grandchildren and seeing what changes are in store for them.

And last but not least, thank you, Greenleaf, for taking on this project and giving me your trust and support. A special thanks to Liz Brown—as my editor you had wonderful ideas and were extremely helpful in getting my first-draft manuscript organized.

Notes

Section One: Careers in Today's World

1. Douglas T. Hall, *Careers in Organizations* (Pacific Palisades, CA: Goodyear, 1976), 2.

2. Donald E. Super and Jean Pierre Jordaan, "Career Development Theory," *British Journal of Guidance & Counselling,* Vol. 1, Issue 1 (1973): 3–16, doi:10.1080/03069887308259333.

3. Douglas T. Hall, "The Protean Career: A Quarter-Century Journey," School of Management Boston University, June 2003.

4. Gallup, *State of the American Workforce: Employee Engagement Insights for U.S. Business Leaders* (2013), http://www.gallup.com/services/178514/state-american-workplace.aspx.

5. Frances Hesselbein and Eric K. Shinseki, *Be, Know, Do: Leadership the Army Way, adapted from the Official Army Leadership Manual* (San Francisco, CA: Jossey-Bass, 2004).

6. Richard N. Bolles, *What Color Is Your Parachute? 2009 A Practical Manual for Job-Hunters and Career-Changers* (Berkeley: Ten Speed Press, 2009).

Section Two: Who's Seeking Work?

1. Dan Primack, "Exclusive: George Zimmer on Being Fired by Men's Wearhouse, and What's Next," *Fortune*, December 9, 2013, http://fortune.com/2013/12/09/exclusive-george-zimmer-on-being-fired-by-mens-wearhouse-and-whats-next/.

2. Employee Benefit Research Institute and Sudipto Banerjee, "Trends in Retirement Satisfaction in the United States," *Notes*, April 2016, Vol. 37, No. 4, https://www.ebri.org/pdf/notespdf/EBRI_Notes_04_Apr16.Ret-Satis.pdf.

Section Four: Workplace Strategies

1. Amy Adkins, "What Millennials Want From Work and Life," Gallup, May 11, 2016, http://www.gallup.com/businessjournal/191435/millennials-work-life.aspx.

2. Howard Schultz and Joanne Gordon, *Onward: How Starbucks Fought for Its Life without Losing Its Soul* (West Sussex: Wiley & Sons, 2011).

3. Robert Hogan, Joyce Hogan, and Rodney Warrenfeltz, *The Hogan Guide: Interpretation and Use of the Hogan Inventories* (Tulsa, OK: Hogan Assessment Systems, 2007), 16.

4. Marisa Kendall, "2011 Graduates Finding a Better Job Market," *USA Today*, April 22, 2011, http://usatoday30.usatoday.com/money/economy/employment/2011-04-21-college-grad-job-market.htm.

5. Lawrence Katz and Alan Krueger, "The Rise and Nature of Alternative Work Arrangements in the United States, 1995–2015," March 29, 2016, http://scholar.harvard.edu/files/lkatz/files/katz_krueger_cws_v3.pdf?m=1459369766.

6. Henry Kimsey-House, Karen Kimsey-House, Philip Sandahl, and Laura Whitworth, *Co-Active Coaching: Changing Business, Transforming Lives* (Boston, MA: Nicholas Brealey, 2011).

7. Phillippa Lally, Cornelia H. M. Van Jaarsveld, Henry W. W. Potts, and Jane Wardle, "How Are Habits Formed: Modelling Habit Formation in the Real World," *European Journal of Social Psychology*, 2010, Volume 40, Issue 6.

8. *Feedback in Performance Reviews*, Center for Creative Leadership, Ideas Into Action Guidebooks, 2011.

9. Marshall Goldsmith, *What Got You Here Won't Get You There* (New York: Hyperion, 2007).

10. http://unabridged.merriam-webster.com/unabridged/competence.

11. "Two-Thirds of People Consider Diversity Important When Deciding Where to Work," Glassdoor Survey, Press Release, November 17, 2014, https://www.glassdoor.com/press/twothirds-people-diversity-important-deciding-work-glassdoor-survey-2/.

12. Sara Murray, "GM's Promotion of Barra to CEO a Breakthrough for Women," *The Wall Street Journal,* December 10, 2013, http://www.wsj.com/articles/SB10001424052702303330204579250831938560544.

13. "Words of Wisdom from Warren Buffett," *AARP The Magazine*, August/September 2013, http://www.aarp.org/money/investing/info-08-2013/warren-buffett-on-money-success.html.

Section Five: Personal Growth Strategies

1. Robert Witherspoon and Randall P. White, *Four Essential Ways That Coaching Can Help Executives* (Greensboro, NC: Center for Creative Leadership, 1997).

2. Mark Berman, "Watch Jill Abramson's Commencement Speech at Wake Forest," *Washington Post*, May 19, 2014, https://www.washingtonpost.com/news/post-nation/wp/2014/05/19/watch-jill-abramsons-commencement-speech-at-wake-forest/.

3. Marilee C. Goldberg, "Expert Question Asking: The Engine of Successful Coaching," *The Manchester Review*, 1998. Reprint 990401.

4. Carol Dweck, *Mindset: The New Psychology of Success* (New York: Ballantine, 2008).

5. William Bridges, *Managing Transitions: Making the Most of Change* (Reading, MA: Perseus Books, 1991), 99–100.

6. Tim Gallwey, *The Inner Game of Work* (New York: Random House, 2000).

7. Robert Kegan and Lisa Lahey, "The Real Reason People Won't Change," *Harvard Business Review*, November 2001, https://hbr.org/2001/11/the-real-reason-people-wont-change.

8. Jason Zweig, "The Secrets of Berkshire's Success: An Interview with Charlie Munger," *The Wall Street Journal*, September 12, 2014, http://www.wsj.com/articles/the-secrets-of-berkshires-success-an-interview-with-charlie-munger-1410543815.

About the Author

Jim Ward, MA, PCC, is a seasoned human resources executive and professional coach with over twenty-five years' experience working with individuals and corporations to solve their business and human capital issues. Having had the benefit of living and working in Asia for many years during his corporate career, Jim understands the importance of diversity, cultural sensitivity, and globalization. He has a master's degree in human resource management and completed the Columbia Coaching Certificate Program at Columbia University. His company, New Directions Consulting, provides coaching and human capital strategies to corporations and individuals. He lives in Southern California and is married with two adult sons. In his spare time he is a recreational triathlete (albeit a slow one). He can be reached at www.new-directions.org or at Jim@new-directions.org.